MORE WRESTLING
THAN DANCING

MORE WRESTLING
THAN DANCING

An autobiography

David Moreau

Hutchinson
London Sydney Auckland Johannesburg

This edition first published in 1990 by
Hutchinson

Century Hutchinson Ltd,
20 Vauxhall Bridge Road, London, SW1V 2SA

Century Hutchinson Australia (Pty) Ltd,
20 Alfred Street, Milsons Point, Sydney NSW 2061, Australia

Century Hutchinson New Zealand Limited,
PO Box 40–086, Glenfield, Auckland 10, New Zealand

Century Hutchinson South Africa (Pty) Ltd,
PO Box 337, Bergvlei 2012, South Africa

British Library Cataloguing in Publication Data
Moreau, David
    More wrestling than dancing.
    1. Great Britain. Journalism – Biographies
    I. Title
    070.92

ISBN 0–09–173923–3

Photoset by Speedset Ltd, Ellesmere Port
Printed and bound in Great Britain by
Butler and Tanner Ltd, Frome, Somerset

For Reg, Winnie and Prinia

1

Long before I read St Exupéry's *Wind, Sand and Stars* with tears in my teenaged eyes, I had the strong impression that, one day, I would take to the air. I remember as if it was yesterday the day that I first put my airmanship to the test.

A rather forward East African three-year-old at the time, heavily influenced by my sister Prinia nearly two years older, I was standing in my short pants on the broad stone balustrade of our corrugated-iron-roofed bungalow at Amani, in what was then Tanganyika, East Africa. Fifty miles to the east and four thousand lower, the Indian Ocean gleamed blue, the shark-fin shaped sails of the Arab dhows visible on it to those with exceptional eyesight.

'Go on,' said my sister, 'just wave your arms up and down. You'll be all right.' Looking back now, the tensions of sibling rivalry may have been at work in her, and perhaps she saw this as the Final Solution to the tiresome younger brother problem. But that didn't occur to me at the time.

I shuffled my tiny sandals to the edge of the stonework, swung my cupped palms up and down as powerfully as I could, gained my courage by emitting the sound of a revving engine and leapt into the twelve foot void. As a good pilot should, I had planned my circuit before taking off. I would flap my way effortlessly over the rose bed and the hibiscus hedge, then do my final approach and let down stylishly with shock-absorbing bent knees on the dirt road beyond.

It did not work out quite as planned. Like a hundredweight of discarded ballast, I plummeted straight down towards the recently pruned, infinitely spiky-looking roses. At the last moment, by a feat of airmanship, I managed to bank to the left enough to avoid the insertion of a neatly sawn stem into my backside. But I could not miss the trowel which lay abandoned alongside, and I thumped down on its sharp edge. I seemed to see a fleeting look of triumph on my sister's face just before impact, and I began transmitting a shrill Mayday caterwauling even before my feet became embedded in the Amani loam.

'I'll go and get Mummy,' shouted my sister as I keeled belatedly into the impact-absorbing position favoured nowadays by parachutists. Mummy duly arrived from her bath, dripping and towelled, and her concept of First Aid was to drop me fully clad into the hot water to ease the pain. I remember that my floppy grey felt hat shrank instantly to my head, like part of the Iron Maiden.

Strangely enough, that first crash landing did not completely cure me of a desire for aerial manoeuvres. Below the house to the east was a small wood, full of unfriendly little snakes. One of the trees sported huge, squashy brown fruit, which, when they fell from a height, burst with a shower of grumulous brown matter, as if it was raining cottage pies. This eerie fruit drew us, and, one day about a year later, we toiled our way up the frail branches at the bottom, and on to the more substantial ones higher up. As we reached up to each junction on the bole, we felt cautiously for scorpions, spitting snakes, or the giant ants known as siafu. East African children grow up used to living in a world full of menace. Even our unoccupied gumboots usually disgorged small yellow land crabs if shaken upside down before being put on.

Finally, we climbed out of the green jungle dimness, and into the hot sunlight higher up. Out at the end of a thick branch, I saw a tempting cluster of cottage pie fruit. I began to edge my way towards it. My more prudent sister stayed by the trunk to watch me. I cannot now say exactly what happened as I neared my booty, but one minute I was reaching out for a massive brown gourd, and the next, I was in an ugly power dive towards the jungle undergrowth. This time, because I fell an estimated thirty five feet, there was time enough for me to review a substantial part of my short life to date before I hit the ground with a thud and bounced in the air again.

I used to recall this feeling later whenever I saw stunt men or their dummies in films falling to their doom off cliffs and skyscrapers. I lost consciousness for a bit, and only came to when I was safely home in the family bungalow. A broken bone in my back was diagnosed, and to distract me from my suffering, I was given a clockwork Zeppelin driven by a mica propeller which circled endlessly round the ceiling light from which it was hung. I lay and watched it for more than a month.

During those eventful five years on a jungle-clad African mountain top, I seemed to spend quite a lot of time in bed, recovering from accidents and various afflictions, and taking undrinkable and largely ineffective medication. For instance, quinine was in those days the only known weapon against malaria. I chewed an appallingly bitter-tasting tablet of it at least every day of my conscious existence, without greatly affecting the constant attacks of wracking fever that the confounded mosquitoes ensured by penetrating the net over my bed most nights, and sinking their grubby proboscises into my young flesh.

Oddly enough, my sojourns in bed did not greatly upset me, as far as I remember, because I loved the arrowroot potion with which I was plied, and there was a constant flow of gifts to forestall boredom. Also, I now realize that it kept me out of the dangerous world outside, and I was probably timid enough to be grateful for that.

In fact we were under constant siege by savage creatures. Some days, the burning noonday sun – we were only 20 minutes south of the equator – would be darkened by huge swarms of locusts. Then, all of us would rush into the garden with sprays of Flit and buckets to bang in an effort to save the pawpaw trees on whose fruit we breakfasted every day, not to mention the flowers and succulents which my mother called her 'darling children'. Other days, there would be a commotion from the garden because someone had observed a two inch wide band of siafu soldier ants marching on the hen run or our private zoo, and they knew that if this implacable army could not be diverted by boiling water and disinfectant, there would be some small skeletons in the cages by nightfall.

One night, my father heard a strange noise under my sister Prinia's bed – she shared a room with him for security reasons, as I did with my mother. Sitting up, he saw a pair of startlingly golden eyes returning his stare from beneath the springs.

'Move over to the other side of your bed, Prinia,' he said

calmly, 'and cover your ears. There's going to be a loud bang.' Seconds later, there was. With two shots of the .38 Smith and Wesson revolver pulled out from under his pillow, he had wounded a leopard which had somehow wormed its way through a small opening of the window. It scrambled back out, and just about survived as far as the edge of the forest.

On another occasion, I went out to the woodshed where we kept the logs that heated the kitchen stove and made the occasional sitting-room fire during the rainy season. On top of the pile of wood was a puff adder, only about five feet long, but with a body as thick as a man's thigh. When it saw me, it began to sway with slow menace. I must have found the movement rather hypnotic, because I stood rooted to the earth floor in my StartRite sandals. Suddenly, Martin, the houseboy, appeared in the doorway, curious to see why such a noisy child had fallen so suddenly silent. He gave a Swahili yell, dragged me out of the way, then belted away to the hall to fetch the special assegai-ended stick that we used for transfixing snakes. I still remember the ugly squelch that the weapon made as he plunged it into the reptile.

We were not usually allowed to walk about outside without some kind of footgear because of a really horrible creature called the chigger. For some reason, this nested in the corners of the nails on your toes if given the opportunity, and then the only thing to be done was to prise its eggs out with the end of a large, heated safety pin, before they produced an even more painful larva.

One night, I said to my mother just as I was getting drowsy, 'Mummy, what's that rustling noise in the ceiling?'

'It's all right, darling,' she answered reassuringly, 'it's only a snake keeping down the rat population up there.' She always seemed to be very laid back about the insects that she invariably referred to as 'doods'. Things the size of small pterodactyls seemed to me to be cruising about in the sky sometimes, but she gave them scant attention. And she was nearly as good as my father at dealing with unexpected beasts. Once, clutching a pillow, she went to investigate an odd noise in the sitting-room. When she opened the door, she found a full grown mongoose engaged in pushing the ornaments off the mantelshelf. It looked as if it might attack her, so she clouted it with the pillow, and it ran off on to the verandah.

In the steamy climate, with endless sunshine and a fertile soil, everything grew in abundance. A stick pushed into the ground seemed to develop leaves in a few days. And my father was sitting one day on the sofa, when he felt his backside getting warm. Shortly, a bud from a kapok seed burst out through the open weave of the material. Somehow, in germinating, it had generated enough heat to scorch the fabric.

At meals, my parents sometimes drank a brown liquid which was generated in a washbasin in the spare room. Some kind of fleshy, pearl-coloured fungus grew in it, nourished by them with cold tea and spoonfuls of sugar. The result, after maturing briefly, was like a rather strong cider. I never discovered where the fungus came from or what it was, but it would grow rapidly to fill any vessel it was put in, and smelt like a brewery.

In the shallow valley behind the house was the Bustani, a market garden founded by the German conquerors of the territory. Fruit and vegetables rioted colourfully across it. Jacaranda trees flamed along one side of the bungalow, and beyond them was a small meteorological station. This attempted to cope with a succession of natural phenomena which included hurricanes, three inches of rain in an hour, and earthquakes from the Rift Valley not far away which rattled the metal roof and made the lampshades sway.

Our garden crawled with life. There were regiments of grey centipedes up to three inches long, which smelt horrible when stamped on, and also large black scorpions which paraded about with their lethal tails over their heads with the same apparent pride that retriever dogs show when they have got hold of one of your best slippers.

Once, when we were walking along the bank of the Pangani River a few miles away, I tripped and sprawled with a shriek over what I thought was a branch hidden in the long grass. It proved, in fact, to be the tail of a large crocodile, which lashed its bruised appendage vigorously twice, then raced off on its fat little legs to splash into the water, as green and greasy as the Limpopo.

One day, during a picnic in a coffee shamba, I decided to climb one of the dark-leaved bushes to get at the bright red fruit that holds the prized bean. Halfway up, I struck something that broke over my head like rotten earthenware. Suddenly, I was crawling with the small red ants whose nest I had shattered. Enraged, they injected a near-lethal dose of formic acid into me, and I rapidly swooned. My parents thought for a bit that it was all over, but, after an hour or two of toxic shock, I seemed to be none the worse.

To the south of our house, the dusty road led to the top of the mountain where my father's office was. At a junction of the ways stood an attractive bush called an Allspice Tree, out of which my sister fell and broke her arm when aged about six. The rough scree-clad outcrop behind the bush was known as Lion Hill, because a fine specimen had once been seen brooding up there. We never saw him again, but the grunting and roaring of the huge cats could often be heard in the forest a few hundred yards away.

Thinking about the adventures that were crammed into our five short years in Tanzania, I think it was probably remarkable that we survived at all. And I wonder what it must be like for parents to bring up children in conditions in which you never know what is going to attack them next.

2

My father, Reginald Ernest Moreau, was born in 1897, the only son of a modest middle-class family in Kingston-on-Thames. The Moreau name had come over from France after the 1848 Revolution, and the youngish couple of refugees had then set up as booksellers in Bayswater. I rather doubt whether the elegantly bemoustached French intellectual would ever have expected to end up buried anywhere as unremarkable as Norbiton churchyard.

My great-grandfather, Adolphe Moreau, still looked very French, as did my equally powerfully moustached grandfather, Paul Moreau. Obviously the Gallic genes survived very strongly, and may have some connection with my own passion for France and the French.

My father's mother came from Trade – she was the daughter of a robust family of bakers that had a popular shop at Number 6 the Apple Market in Kingston-on-Thames. Perhaps the most remarkable thing about the family was that Uncle Willie savoured so many of his own cakes that he ended up weighing thirty-seven stone, having difficulty in getting through doors, and in finding beds that would bear his stupendous bulk for a whole night.

My father proved to be very bright at school, and not wholly devoid of athletic prowess – he won a medal at the age of fifteen for swimming a mile in the Thames, a feat which nowadays would oblige you to have your stomach pumped out.

Very early, he began to take an interest in botany, zoology, and, most particularly, birds. Being myopic from childhood, he took very early to binoculars so as to be able to study them more intently. While still at school, he travelled all over Southern England on a bicycle, developing impressive calf muscles in the process, to watch rare birds, and to indulge his other passion of exploring castles and churches.

By the time that he left school, the family had fallen on hard times, because Paul Moreau, his prosperous stockbroker father, had been hit by a swinging train door as it flashed through Surbiton station. The consequent severe head injuries meant that he never worked again, and, indeed, they sent him rather potty. My grandmother held the family together by gallantly working and taking in lodgers, but my father was not able to fulfil his dream of going to a major university, which he was otherwise quite clever enough to have done. In fact, fifty years later, he was awarded an honorary degree in zoology at Oxford, the Public Orator of the time making a witty Latin speech packed with onomatopoeia about his discoveries in ornithology.

So, at seventeen, he joined the War Office in the Exchequer and Audit Department as a clerk. Sometimes he commuted up to Whitehall on his bicycle. Otherwise it was a steam train to Waterloo, followed by a horsedrawn tram, with straw on the floor to keep the passengers' feet warm in winter.

The work was monotonous for someone with his taste for adventure and open country, and, shortly after the First World War broke out, he asked for a transfer to the much more glamorous branch of the office in Cairo, Egypt. This move was also motivated by the fact that he had begun to suffer from the family disease of arthritis, which had already put a young aunt into a wheelchair for life. A doctor, treating him with an enlightenment unusual so early in this century, had extracted some tissue from one of his inflamed big toe joints, cultured it into an auto-vaccine, and given it as a series of desensitising injections. This had produced some improvement, but the same man had said that my father's best hope of avoiding severe disability would be to emigrate to a hot climate and stay there.

Once in Egypt, he began to behave like the Indiana Jones character that he had clearly always wanted to be. Adopting a bush hat, khaki shirt and shorts and Lotus Veldtschoen, he learned quite good Arabic, and began making long journeys by ancient car, rail, and on foot into the surrounding desert. He took to flies, protesting camels, leather water bottles and Bedouin as if Kingston-on-Thames had never existed.

His staid office colleagues regarded him as a harmless crank.

But he rapidly gained recognition from the scientific journals in Britain for his meticulous papers on bird migration and the habits of the desert wild life. One of the more frequent publishers of his work at this time was the *Ibis*, the journal of the British Ornithologists' Union, which later he was to edit for eleven years.

He took to keeping pets. One of them was a baby bittern, given him as a bedraggled bundle of feathers by an Arab who knew his reputation as Abu Nadaar – Father of the Glasses – and friend of feathered folk. It rapidly grew into a large bird, and his French landlady rather surprisingly tolerated its gong-like booming in the early hours of the morning.

Then one day my father was stricken with paratyphoid and hospitalized. He insisted on taking his bird with him. It was a big Army establishment, full of stately men from the shires, who insisted that their chargers should be brought into the yard at regular intervals, so that they could stand swaying on the balconies in their hospital-issue pyjamas and gravely salute their equine friends.

They did not take kindly to this young, bespectacled captain and the confounded bird that woke everyone at the first sign of dawn. Eventually a Scots doctor said that if my father could not devise a means of keeping his awful bird under control, he would personally wring its neck. Huffily and rather unsteadily, my father discharged himself with his fine specimen of *Botaurus stellaris*, and it continued to be his inseparable companion for years.

One day in the early 1920s, leafing through the details of desert outposts that were getting supplies from the British Army in Cairo, my father noted that a certain Captain Austin Kennett was one of the beneficiaries. He lived among a remote collection of huts at Kingi, many miles down the desert railway line towards Mersa Matruh. With the bureaucratic stroke of the pen which he had learned from his superiors, my father cut off the Kingi supplies.

A few days later, a pitiful appeal arrived via a camel messenger. The men, women and children were faced with real hardship, even starvation, by the cutting off of their British Army rations. Delighted at the thought of a desert business trip

9

right in the middle of passerine bird migration time, my father donned his bush hat and binoculars, and set off on the single track railway to Kingi.

At the far end, he trudged the mile from the halt on the line, and finally arrived at the tiny settlement. The first person that he met was a fragrant white creature, dressed, as the photographs of the time reveal, in a voluminous, pale garment and floppy felt hat to protect her from the harmful rays of the sun.

She was, he discovered, the daughter of a Cumbrian vicar, who had come out a year before to act as nursemaid to the Kennetts' son, John England. The latter, aged only about five, clearly remembers the arrival of my father, accompanied by an alarmingly large bird.

Once they had settled the little matter of avoiding being starved, the young officer and the nursemaid took a walk in the desert, and discovered that they shared a passion for the spring flowers of the sandy wastes, as well as birds and mammals, such as the jerboas and long-eared desert foxes, one of which was the nursemaid's devoted pet. And, by the time that it was necessary for the young captain to run painfully on his arthritic ankles to catch the solitary train smoking towards the halt, it was certain that they could hardly wait to meet again.

Accounts from the time make it clear that, although my mother, Winifred Muriel (for it was she), had had the refined upbringing of a Victorian country vicar's daughter, she could also be a real tearaway. At Kingi, for example, there was a camel-drivers' strike one day. My mother happened to be alone on the station at the time, and the situation looked quite serious. The men were clustered in an ugly mood in front of the high gate to the official bungalow. My mother climbed on one of the gate posts, nearly eight feet high, and ramming her felt hat on her head, jumped down into the middle of the assembled men, draperies flying, and shouting as she fell, 'Go back to work at once, do you hear?' They duly did.

The little boy that she was looking after there remembers that one night a burglar came stealthily into their bedroom. Biding her time until he was busy rummaging in a cupboard, she suddenly sat up with an eldritch shriek, then flew across the room in her nightdress to belabour the intruder with her fists. As he fled, a knife tinkled to the floor.

On another occasion, the two of them were in a horsedrawn taxi in Cairo, when the driver diverted from the route that he should have taken, and started rapidly off for the native quarter. Suspecting his motives, my mother pointed out that they did not want to go that way. The driver answered angrily, and kept on, whipping up his horse.

'When I give you the signal,' whispered my mother conspiratorially to her charge, 'jump down and run immediately to that last bridge over the Nile. I'll meet you there in a minute or two.'

He did as he was told, and as his little legs were carrying him away, he glanced back and saw his ladylike nursemaid leap agilely on to the driver's box and begin belabouring him with her bunched fists, before dropping to the ground and following the little lad at a run.

A couple of years after they first met in this remote place, Winnie and Reg came home to England for his leave, and were married at the church in Cumbria where her father had officiated, by a man known in family history only as 'little Proud'. After a honeymoon in the Lepontine Alps, they went back by ship from Venice to Egypt, and began living in a large tent on the edge of the desert at Maadi. In due course, my sister Prinia was born. Her name came from the Prinia Gracilis bird, that was nesting at the top of one of the tent poles at the time.

I followed twenty months later. My father wanted to call me Buphagus, the Latin name of the ox pecker, because he thought it rolled off the tongue in a virile fashion. There can be little doubt that it would have been a useful name for standing out in a crowd, but my mother dissuaded him in time.

We did not stay in Egypt for very long after that. My father's outstanding gifts as a scientific observer and cataloguer had been noticed, and he was offered the job as Secretary of the East African Agricultural Research Institute more than two thousand miles further south in what was then Tanganyika. I dimly remember crooning excitedly over my first birthday present – a miniature tin model of a 1927 vintage gas stove – among the unclad floor timbers of the corrugated-iron-roofed bungalow which was being built for the family at Amani.

3

The luminous skies and terracotta hills of Africa gave me a brightly coloured patchwork in my mind that sustained me through the grey imprisonment of my later schooling in England. I remember as a six-year-old feeling quite sorry for the lads from Gidea Park and Bromley who had not seen the 19,000-foot peak of Mount Kilimanjaro glimmering in the mist two hundred miles north of our house; not taken the death-defying drive in the Station's six-wheeler lorry down the brown-walled canyon that led to the power works at Zigi; not seen the scorched savannahs of the Serengeti dotted with more lion, giraffe, vildebeest and zebras than you could see in a lifetime of visiting the London Zoo; and not had one's shorts-clad father come home from the office guffawing helplessly because when he had pulled the chain in the lavatory, a three-foot snake had thumped down on his head.

In fact, I found it quite odd to discover how different the father species in general was from the particular specimen that I had grown up with. For example, thinking that it might be inconvenient to have appendicitis in Darkest Africa, my father had it cut out on one of his trips home, with the same insouciance that most of us might show when having the bonnet lifted on a car to change the plugs. He did the same with his teeth, having them all pulled out, then chomping contentedly with a slightly equine Xylonite set for the rest of his life. I was never quite sure whether he was just naturally brave, or whether a lifetime of rigorous self-control had enabled him to mask fear better than most.

Once, for example, he went on safari up Mount Kilimanjaro and was aware that a large black rhino was following him with hostile intent. Occasionally, he would let off the loud bang of a .38 pistol cartridge over the dark armoured head that loomed behind him, half-hidden in the jungle grass. By nightfall it seemed to have disappeared, and he pitched his small tent, put up his camp bed and climbed into his sleeping bag. A couple of hours later, with a roar like the Flying Scotsman, the slab-sided animal revenged itself by charging through his tent, demolishing everything but leaving him unhurt. When he got back to us at home, the only thing that he complained about was that his breakfast of rice pudding and jam had been hurled from the bedside table into his sleeping bag.

He was probably the only man I have known who seemed to have no fear of animals. Many years later, when the three of us were crossing a field on our way to dig up ammonites on Golden Cap above Lyme Regis, a huge Clydesdale stallion that was loose in it charged at us.

My mother and I raced for the surrounding wall, and swiftly put six feet of stone between us. My father, a placid, scholarly figure in his gold-rimmed spectacles, walked on at a leisurely gait. The ton or two of animal missed him by about eighteen inches, even just the slipstream making him stagger. I heard him say, 'Who's a fierce, wild horsey, then?' The animal turned in a big circle, and swept back for a head-on confrontation. My father beamed amiably at it, and did not deviate. Again, the horse just missed him, then cantered into a distant corner of the field to sulk about this person who did not seem to know the rules. After a decent interval, my mother and I cautiously joined my quite unmoved father.

Although he was quite donnish in his relations with my sister and me, he could also make life very good fun, and he knew how to rescue us from absurd situations. Once, driving in the jungle, a yelling tribesman ran fifty yards, to put his leg over the open side of the car and try to climb in the back with Prinia and me. Shouting 'Umpumbafu!' (the Swahili for idiot), my father gave him an almighty slap on the bare thigh, and, still shouting, the man ran off.

On another occasion, we had embarked in an ancient launch to go round the mangrove swamps on the coast at Mombasa. All kinds of things went wrong; the motor failed, one of our party unwisely leaned over the bow and was leapt at by a gnashing crocodile, which frightened him half to death, and, as night began to fall, a sea started to get up under the influence of a sudden wild wind. My father was very at home in boats and a good oarsman, and he took charge of the situation, hiding me and my sister in the tar-smelling space under the back thwart out of danger from the crocodile and friends, while he oversaw the Indian boatman, stripped to his cache-sexe, as he tried to mend the engine. I was not really frightened as we worked our way slowly back through the dark, haunted clumps of trees growing in the inhospitably muddy water. But my mother was. She had stayed behind in the town, and we arrived back at the house in a rickshaw at 1 a.m., dirty and soaked.

While we were still quite young, I remember hearing my father reciting ribald limericks, which he loved, to visitors to the house. I distinctly recall him hooting over one that ran:

> There once was a Bey of Algiers,
> Who said to his Harem, my dears,
> You may think it oddofme,
> But I've given up sodomy,
> Fornication tonight. Loud cheers.

It took me a few years to find out what all the words meant.

He would also take incurable dislikes to buildings and places, as befitted a man who knew Professor Pevsner's work by heart. On our leaves in England, we sometimes had occasion to drive through a Sussex village with the strange name of The Dicker. He had deep loathing for its straggling ribbon development, and for five minutes after negotiating it, he would roar out a chorus of 'We've passed by The Dicker', to the tune of 'Lloyd George knew my father'.

One of the better entertainments that he devised for us in Africa was the trips down to a German farm in the south of the territory, run by a certain Mrs Krahl. Down there, the sociably two-holer outside lavatory had a fine view of a small, bird-infested lake the other side of its white curtain. For an ornithologist, this was the perfect way of performing one's devoirs.

I also remember that, from there, my sister and I set out in a canvas contraption suspended between two mules to accompany my mother up a nearby mountain. The reason was unexpected – near the top was a nunnery, and one of the nuns was a fine dentist. My mother had gone up to have a few more of her teeth removed. In due course she, like my father, would sport a fine Xylonite set.

Down at Mrs Krahl's, we came into contact with large farm animals for the first time, and they seemed strangely lacking in character when compared with the rampant wild creatures on the savannahs below our mountain home. We also met German missionaries there, one of whom nicknamed me Soupan Kuspott, for no reason that I could divine. He and others like him left me with a lifelong belief that the greatest buffoons are elderly Germans.

Behind our bungalow, my mother got together a small zoo of her own. My sister once counted ninety animals in it, including a monkey which bit poor Prinia on the vaccination mark. There was also a bushbuck, a mongoose and a blue duiker, as well as countless birds, chinchillas and coneys. It was from my mother in those days that I got the habit of apostrophizing furry creatures in an anthropromorphic tone, as if they were fellow small boys. She always reasoned with them, just as some people talk lovably to plants, and often they seemed to sense that she was fiercely concerned for them, and they would be untypically co-operative.

She could also indulge in the same strongarm methods that had already surprised Egyptian blackguards. Once she saw a Bateleur Eagle – the largest bird in the world, with a ten-foot wingspan – busy disembowelling the Rhode Island Reds that she kept in a run at the back of the house to supply us with eggs.

'Just you wait,' she snarled, snatching up a sack and propelling her slight 5-foot-1-inch frame through the rickety door of the hen run. The surprised eagle had no time to begin its lumbering take-off run across the beaten red earth before she seized it by the feathery scruff and rammed it beak first into the hessian. She paid no attention at all to its razor-sharp talons, bigger than a man's hand, nor the wildly remonstrating bill. The silently terrified audience of my sister and myself applauded as she marched out of the hen run with the huge marauder screaming and struggling in his prison. The roadman Pigawashi, who was always appointed by my father to keep an eye on us when he was away on safari, was duly handed the Bateleur, with instructions to release it deep in the surrounding jungle.

Because she was always nurturing tragic little nestlings that had baled prematurely out of their nests in the tall rain forest trees all round, my mother often wore an old sock between her bosoms with a scrap of bird life keeping warm in it. She was perfectly capable of going out to dinner in a low-cut dress in this configuration, and on one occasion sat next to the Governor of the Province, who laughed until tears rolled down his weather-beaten face when he realized that the strangled cheeping that could be heard above the rustle of polite conversation emanated from between the breasts of the young woman sitting on his left.

My father became more like Indiana Jones than ever. By now he had begun to write short stories partly based on his adventures, hammering them out on a 1912 Corona that he always said was part of the Sack of Constantinople. Half a century later, I discovered that the poet Christopher Fry has done his life's work on an identical device. Some of my father's tales won awards, and he also published a collection of them through Jonathan Cape under the title *The Temple Servant*.

One of the side-effects of the modest economic success of his literary career was that he bought a succession of two-cylinder air-cooled Jowett cars. They could not boil while struggling uphill in the hot season, and also had a big ground clearance. In them, we used to roam round the rutted forest tracks looking for adventures.

My father would also go off on foot for weeks on genuine safaris. Armed with a rifle, with which he was a very good shot despite his glasses, he was accompanied by an askari called Salimu. He also went with another bush-hatted friend called Tom Baldock, who lived in a small boma on a remote, thorny mountain top a few miles away. Sometimes they put up hides in the forest, and in these they would sit devotedly for weeks, being consumed by mosquitoes, while studying birds such as the Hornbill. They shot unusual birds that they saw, and sent their skins to the Bird Room at the British Museum for classification. Because the state of the birds' breeding organs was significant, my father always examined them attentively, and in due course he acquired the local nickname 'Professor Gonad'.

These collecting and observing activities rapidly brought him scientific recognition; a weaver bird he discovered was called *Moreaui* after him, and another avian was given the name *Winifredae* after my mother. A louse, discovered asleep in one of the birds nests that he examined, was also called after him.

My father had always had socialist leanings, and he related very simply and straightforwardly to men and women of all colours. Throughout his life, many people found his eccentricity rather endearing. For example, when already in his sixties, he tried to get on a bus in southern Spain. When he saw it was full, he volunteered to travel on the roof rack, and did a journey over the Sierras for ninety miles perched among the baskets up there. The other passengers applauded the mad Englishman when he eventually climbed stiffly down again.

My mother also, as a former pillar of Vicarage tea parties, could talk to practically anyone about almost anything. This facility was useful in dealing with the rather numerous staff. At any one time, we usually had a houseboy, cook, dhobi and a gardener, although their total monthly wage was only a few Tanganyika shillings, with holes in the middle so that they could be conveniently threaded on a piece of string.

Prinia and I picked up quite a lot of Swahili, and it seemed natural to talk about the lavatory as the *cho*, the car as a *gharri*, insects as *wadudu*, a man as an *mtu* – with the plural *watu* – and so on. If the boys – some of whom were quite elderly – did not understand our garblings, they would just stand giggling helplessly until someone rescued them.

Like most isolated children, Prinia and I developed a dialect of neologisms which has stayed with us, and, indeed, been passed on down the family. A series of concentric circles, as in RAF wing markings, is a 'dororumpti', which still seems to me quite a neat and somehow onomatopoeic summary. Various forms of vehicle that could be dragged or pushed were called 'trolliollyaxles'. Moving about on your heels with your toes pointing in the air at an angle of 45 degrees was 'walking on your or-ors'. Deep, grinding massage of a muscle such as the bicep or thight, was 'groggling.' Any kind of wind instrument was a 'toofal'. It made it possible to have a conversation which would be largely incomprehensible to strangers.

To my young eyes, all the other whites on this remote mountain top had well-defined characters. Nutman, down the Dark Path a few hundred feet below us, always had a raffish look, and nowadays I would imagine him putting his hand up ladies' skirts at every opportunity. Further away lived Peter Greenaway, whose uniform of tweeds, solar topee, gold-rimmed spectacles and vasculum betokened a fine nine-teenth-century-style naturalist. Our nearest neighbours, the Nowells, who directed the Institute, always seemed unimagin-ably old, and they were probably nearly fifty. The Worsleys, who lived higher up near the laboratories, I always thought of as rather wealthy, probably because they toured about in a glittering Humber, rather than the tattered Ford Boxbodies that most of the rest clattered about in. In fact, when I was only eighteen months old, this Humber had nearly been my undoing. Clasped in the arms of my ayah, and dressed in swaddling clothes for some odd maternal reason, I saw this brightly shining vision, hood stylishly down, bobbing down the ruts past our bungalow. Easily maddened then, as now, by the sight of a really splendid vehicle, I cried 'Mticar', kicked excitedly, and volplaned out of the window, my draperies steering me accurately, like the fins of a fat little bomb, towards the concrete gulley twelve feet below. The subsequent day or two of unconsciousness for me were doubtless a relief for my parents from my car-spotting.

The only shop in Amani was the Indian *duka* in the upper level. It carried a weird assortment of goods, and, if you could not manage on what it offered, then you had to bump down into the valley and the junction town of Korogwe, or on to the Indian Ocean breezes at Tanga on the coast. Or you could do what my mother did – choose seductive items from the voluminous catalogue of the Army and Navy Stores, and wait an excited eternity for their arrival by surface mail. No schooling was provided locally, and yet my mother somehow managed to teach us to read and write and do arithmetic to a family standard that put us at no disadvantage when school began in earnest back in England. I am not conscious of spending any time at all than in learning.

Three times during my time in Africa, we came home on leave, travelling on purple-grey Union Castle liners with evocative names like *Dunluce Castle* or *Llandovery Castle*. Once we went round the Cape, and I was shown the spectacular sight of the cloud-capped Table Mountain. And twice we came through the Suez Canal, the heat and flies being very burdensome when only brass ceiling fans attempted the impossible task of keeping you cool. On one occasion we steamed past the fuming black bulk of the volcano Stromboli, looking for all the world as if a giant child had dropped one of its more interesting toys into the blue depths of the Mediterranean.

I had another of my curious accidents on board ship, which has scarred me slightly to this day. Lying on the top bunk in our cabin, feeling very green as the ship crashed and thudded its way through the Bay of Biscay, I suddenly became weightless as we went down a giant wave, and sailed over the rail at the side of the bunk, to land headfirst on the blue rimmed china nightpot that stood expectantly on the hard floor below. I remember tinkling shards, and being hurried through to the ship's doctor as my life blood dribbled on the deck planks so that five stitches could be inserted in my carefully shaved scalp.

To console me after this episode, one of our fellow passengers, a Mr Ruggles, gave me an athletic little dog from the barber's shop which leapt about and yapped when a rubber bulb was squeezed. In his honour, I called it Mr Ruggles, and that night begged my mother to take it to bed with her so that she could appreciate its qualities too. In the morning, to an astonished breakfast saloon of dignified British Colonial Servants, I repeatedly shouted the news that 'Mummy took Mr Ruggles to bed last night.'

I can quite see why cruises become so addictive to some people. There is this captive society about you day and night, to prey on if you are so minded. Inventive ship's officers think up distractions like Crossing the Line to ward off boredom, and every port brings new smells, noises, and adventures. In my day there were glass-bottomed boats at Suez or Mombasa, and lighters that came alongside with yelling vendors of native goods and jongleurs in ports southwards from Naples. As the ship swung at anchor at night, passing logs and small boats

19

occasionally thudded against the metal hull, and you could hear the hissing of steam cranes and winches as shouting men unloaded cargoes.

Finally, aged only five but, it seemed, with half a lifetime of experiences behind me, I came home for good. We moved into my Grandmother's house in Farnham, Surrey, the genteel antithesis of the adventure playground that Prinia and I had enjoyed in East Africa.

Every room there had its characteristic scent. The front room smelt of soot and elderly damask, with a touch of lavender. The dining room was redolent of the horticultural operations that went on in the conservatory that led off it. The cellar hummed with the vegetables that had grown old in it down the years. And the back kitchen smelt of the solvents and glue that my poor old grandad used there as he pottered about making things in a vain attempt to find something to live for. I did not realize for a long time that the dear old man was chronically depressed. The damage to his brain meant that he rarely left the house, and his management was a problem to my red-haired grandmother. Loud noises, such as I probably made all the time, alarmed him, and he was haunted by the fear that we children would fall down the cellar stairs, impale ourselves on his garden implements or letter spikes, or set fire to him or ourselves. He clearly had no concept of what we had already survived in the Dark Continent.

4

Few children in extreme youth reflect whether they actually like their parents or not. They are just there, it seems, to cuddle you if you are lucky; nourish you; put Elastoplast on your lesser wounds, and plan your day so that boredom and aimlessness are avoided as far as possible.

Perhaps the first time that I realized how fond I was of these two not very big and raffishly dressed people – my father with a green editorial eyeshade permanently hoisted above his spectacles, and crumpled shorts above his grey ankle socks; and my mother with a cloche hat pulled down to her eyebrows to replace the African solar topee, a hankie tucked into an ivory bangle, and round-toed shoes like nursery StartRites – was when, one summer day in 1933, they announced that they were going back to Africa without us. This bombshell was dropped at the end of their six months' leave, which we had spent in our inimitably restless family fashion wandering about Cornwall, Scotland and Wales in a huge old convertible Austin 16 with a rattling starting handle.

Probably my parents were determined to make our last real leave together memorable, and they certainly succeeded. In Cornwall we had gone to stay with my mother's sister Mary, who I suppose nowadays would have been regarded as an unrequited lesbian. She had moved into a thirty-room rectory at Liskeard, in adoration of a Mrs Bradwell, a domineering, coarse-grained Irishwoman who was married to a shrunken little cleric. Unfortunately, all the family treasures from my mother's side had funnelled down to Mary, including, it was claimed, thirty teasets, two pianos and a priceless geological collection stemming from Great Uncle Sedgwick, who was for fifty-three years Woodwardian Professor of Geology at Cambridge. And, because the household was so hard up, they lived by selling Mary's family heirlooms until there were none left.

Of course, aged six, I knew nothing of all this. But I did notice that they had an uncountable pack of dogs, which finally grew to about thirty before she died. They would rave through the house, knocking things over, and chewing away at what remained of the Regency furniture. I remember, too, finding some nameless material at the bottom of a glass of milk, and never again ate anything there until I had examined it for detritus.

An important part of this sort of holiday was going for 'explorey' walks. My mother would tell us what rarities we were to look for botanically – perhaps the blue Grass of Parnassus, the Orange Hawkweed, the Sundew or the Pheasant's Eye – and we would compete fiercely to see who could spot them first. My father would tell us what we should look for in the bird world – Gannets, Black-Backed Gulls, Puffins or Willow Warblers – and here too we would keep a keen look-out. Since my father had always read the history of any towns or villages that we went through, this added greatly to their interest. He was particularly fascinated by megaliths and Bronze Age earthwork castles, so that we always detoured from our routes in order to avoid missing sites like the Cheesewring, or Yarnbury and Maiden Castles.

In Scotland, we went to stay in a farmhouse which looked down from the heathery hills on to the Crinan Canal in Argyllshire. Apart from searching for Golden Eagles, Choughs and lost Stormy Petrels, my father borrowed one of the rowing boats that he loved so much, and we pulled round the bay in fair weather and foul. His compact physique and large chest made him strong enough to be able to row all day if necessary, and we would often spend hours in the green waters of the bay with a spinner trailing behind the boat to catch mackerel.

Both my parents also had a very wide acquaintance, so that our stays in bed-and-breakfast establishments and small hotels up and down the country were interspersed by sojourns in patrician houses. I vaguely remember the high polish of everything, the displays of silver, and the polite men- and maidservants, but the only thing that really struck me was the time that one of our hostesses – could it have been a Bonham Carter? – was thought by my mother to be crying about the death of a favourite bull, but in reality it somehow turned out to be her husband who had croaked his last words. And in another house in the Cotswolds, I remember the lavatory being flushed by the use of a thing like a huge brass stirrup pump, said to date from the eighteenth century. I played with it for a long time until dragged away.

Finally my parents told Prinia and me that they had decided that in order to ensure that we were properly educated, as well as to avoid our suffering from the crippling bane of endless malaria, they would be leaving us behind in England. Our guardians would be my godfather, Ronald, and his wife Lilian. They would look after us as if we were their own children.

In due course, surrounded by piles of tattered luggage, my father and mother swung away in their taxi towards Tilbury Docks and their Union Castle liner. Prinia and I looked tearfully round-eyed at each other, overwhelmed that our time as the Memsahib and Bwana Kidogo had come so swiftly to an end. But our self-pity did not last long, and we quickly came to terms with life under Ronald and Lilian's roof, preparing to go to our first boarding school.

Although we called them Uncle and Aunt at their request, neither was a real relative. Ronald was a small, dark, highly intelligent man who smoked incessantly – it eventually killed him. I can still hear the way that he coughed and spluttered his way round the house in Mecklenburgh Square, Bloomsbury, in the mornings.

He had been an Army signaller in the Middle East Army under Allenby during the first Great War, and he was to be Colonel in charge of the Army Exchequer and Audit Department in Egypt during the second one. He was really a frustrated writer, enormously widely read and cultured, but he never really bloomed as he should have done. The only literary item that I remember him actually producing was a neat little poem entitled 'The Blackout', which was the winning entry in a competition for parents at my prep school.

I am afraid that his lack of artistic achievement may have been partly due to Aunt Lilian. A jerkily angular woman, still handsome although snowy-haired, she often poked fun at him, ending her acerbic sentences with a mirthless laugh. In adult life, I have observed that this sort of behaviour, combined with a general lack of encouragement, is liable to shrivel up a sensitive chap.

Lilian possessed other notable features. She had, for example, once dislocated her knee, and ever since had worn a curious, spring loaded apparatus under her stocking which we were not allowed to see. Try as we might to surprise it when temporarily discarded, we never succeeded. I also heard that Lilian had once been with her mother, wheeling her about in a bathchair through the steep streets of a town that may have been Penrith. Going into a shop to buy something, she had left the contraption parked against the pavement with the brake on. When she came out a few minutes later, she saw the unroadworthy thing hurtling off down the hill at a full thirty miles an hour, with the old lady bawling for help from within the faded wickerwork. At the time, having just read *The Wind in The Willows*, I imagined she looked rather like Mr Toad, except that I was sure that she would not have been shouting 'Poop, poop'. I am sorry to say that a minute or two later Lilian was motherless.

Perhaps partly because of this awful experience, and the fact that she could not have children herself because she had caught typhoid on her honeymoon and this had perforated her intestine, Lilian was a slightly uncomfortable person to be with, although she was very kind to the two of us.

Prinia and I settled happily into their large Georgian flat, full of antique furniture, books and pewter. It occupied the two top floors of Number 8 in the square, which has now sadly been demolished to make way for part of London University. We even had maids, a succession of gormless blondes from Lilian's native shire of Cumberland, as it was then. These girls slept in a room kept permanently separated from ours by a locked door. To our delight, Prinia and I discovered that through the crack at the top, we could see them undressing and mutteringly admiring their nude bodies and tweaking their nipples.

Finally, the day came when we went down to the boarding school in Sussex which my parents had selected from the abundant offers addressed to Colonial children in the personal column of *The Times*.

Called Hollington Grange, it was a big, gloomy Victorian pile perched on a knoll in several acres of garden behind St Leonards-on-Sea. The genteel O'Reilly family who kept it consisted of the father, who played the organ in a large church in the town, and had an awesome temper; his wife Honour, who was very intolerant of anything coarse – for example, when the blood orange season came round, we were all obliged to call them rosy oranges. They had four children of their own, the eldest of whom had become organist at Chichester Cathedral while still in his teens.

The other pupils were a motley collection, both in age and background. Some girls and young men already in their twenties seemed to be taken in, while the house's original nursery was occupied by children like me, aged six and upwards, who all devotedly hugged their furry dogs and bears at night.

I think that sex must have begun to rear its ugly head quite shortly afterwards. One of the other occupants of the nursery was a rather older, toothy girl called Pamela, who had been sent home from India with her younger brother Humpy.

She was of a very romantic turn of mind, and, indeed, her favourite game was called 'Loving in the Moonlight'. In pursuit of this, she would thrash about necking on the dead leaves in the remoter bits of shrubbery at any time of the day or night, and with any partners, including myself, that happened along. I do not know whether later she turned into a Good Time, Had by All, but I am certain that Humpy was destined to be a voyeur. He would sit watching his sister's antics from close range, dribbling slightly from a mouth with at least two tombstone front teeth missing, grinning from ear to ear and occasionally lisping encouragement.

I rather envied – at least for a bit – another lad, also called David. His father was a doctor somewhere abroad, and he had obviously decided that he would start young. So he began carrying out medical examinations on the more co-operative of the girls, making them bare the affected part so that he could eye it from all angles before making a definitive diagnosis.

One day in the rabbitry, among all the lovable bunnies that would one day end up in our stews, he was breathily examining a girl called Patricia Harvey-Davies, who had taken off her knickers in the interests of science and furthering his research. Amid the alarmed thumping of the disturbed bunnies, and doubtlessly deafened by his own enthusiasm, he failed to hear the advent of matron, probably alerted to this Hippocratic activity by the jealous Pamela. Anyway, she burst in through the latched door, eyes glittering with anger behind her pebble lenses, and starched cap trembling above her blue uniform.

'I – er, I – er,' the other David was reported to have mouthed in his own defence.

'I can see what you're doing,' she answered grimly, 'and you're a nasty dirty little boy who will be severely punished.'

He was dragged away by the ear in front of the rest of us, to be soundly beaten with a spiky Mason-Pearson hairbrush, while a sniffing Patricia shakenly adjusted her liberty bodice. I no longer envied his particular line of medical practice after that, and, indeed Auntie Honour declared him *persona non grata* shortly afterwards.

One of the more bizarre events in the life of the family at Hollington Grange was the twenty-first birthday party for their eldest son Fergus. The O'Reillys paid for all the guests to dress as Nazi Brownshirts, complete with jackboots and swastika armbands, and Fergus gummed on a toothbrush moustache and dragged a lock of hair over his forehead like his hero Hitler. A bulbous papier mâché head of Hindenburg, with a light inside it, appeared over the house's main entrance, and crimson swastikas were nailed up on the white gateposts down on the road.

I lay in bed in the night nursery, listening to the Horst Wessel song and *Deutschland Über Alles* being roared out, interspersed with continual shouts of *Heil Hitler* and *Sieg Heil*. Later on, some scratchy recordings of the Führer himself were belted out on a gramophone, and I imagined from the cheers that Fergus was earnestly miming to them like a latterday pop star. Shivering in our nursery a few beds away from me lay a little dark-haired German Jewish girl called Joanie, whose father had very wisely whisked her out of the Reich a few months before, after the terrors of *Kristallnacht*.

I often wondered what the very popular O'Reillys and their

equally ecclesiastically oriented friends thought of themselves a few years later when we went to war with the idol of their evening.

The second son had none of these grandiose foibles; in fact, he seemed to be destined to become a voyeur like Humpy. When at home, he was often seen moving noiselessly round in the area of the girls' dormitory and bathrooms, or watching them with a saturnine look on his face as they writhed the swings upwards. There was a general sigh of relief when he joined the Navy.

Apart from classes in arithmetic, reading, writing and French, overseen by the resident schoolmistress, various dramatic performances also took place, accompanied by the family on their chosen instruments. In one, we were various trees. I remember leaping about on the bottom lawn as dusk fell, to the sound of O'Reilly's piano, a fircone strapped to my head, and sylvan green draperies flying from my shoulders. The other children also all incarnated different species of tree, and, into the gathering night, we sang what would now be considered conservationist ditties imploring the heartless woodmen to spare us. I narrowly escaped an entanglement with Pamela as I waited in the shrubbery, clearing my throat, ready to hit a treble note as I came on.

After a year or two, I was judged to have matured enough scholastically to walk into town each day down an unadopted avenue to attend a small local prep school called St Giles. Now that I had acquired two imposing front teeth, I felt that my mature looks were neatly complemented by the school's green and white cap, and I had to be stopped from going to bed in it in case I fractured the peak.

St Giles was my first experience of how lads have to fight in order to establish their exact pecking order in boyish society. On the whole, we took care not to black one another's eyes or break our adversaries' noses, and winding blows to the solar plexus, kicks to the backside, blows to the crutch, and applications of half-nelsons were the usual ways of triumphing. When no staff were watching, there would often be several sets of boys at the same time rolling about and grunting with pain on the grubby parquet.

27

While I was at St Giles, I remember coming to certain conclusions, as hard and fast to-day as they were over fifty years ago. One was that the Bible, with its farrago of battles, violent circumcisions, adultery, betrayals and general desert rampaging, was a strange work for elderly ladies and gentlemen of the sort who taught us to base their well-meaning Divinity lessons on – had they ever really read it? In fact, when I came to think of it, much of conventional religion seemed only credible by the most gullible and the sort of people who in East Africa had believed in witch doctors.

My second resolution, having taken my first and only puff at a cigarette as a nine-year old, was that I should have to be threatened with death by firing squad before I would take another. I couldn't imagine how adults could actually enjoy choking and spluttering over them.

The third was that, having left so much shoe leather on the pavements in and around St Leonards during endless school walks, it was bicycles, cars, roller skates and aeroplanes for me when I grew up, rather than walking a single avoidable step. In fact, I had already made my first vehicle by lashing two sets of wheels off large handcarts to a strong plank. On this I would lie face down steering the front wheels with the small amount of play in the rope that held them on. I called it Horace.

The drives both ways at the Grange were steep and straight, if a little stony, with satisfactory bushes on both sides that could be used as primitive brakes. One day, they failed me, and I zoomed out of the drive gates at 20 m.p.h., and across the main road at the bottom. A terrified, hooting motorist was travelling at right angles to me, and I glimpsed his radiator looming over my head as his brakes screamed. But I beat him by a short head, and plunged unscathed into the berberis hedge on the far side of the road. After that, I was made to dismantle Horace.

Then the Hollington Grange family fell on hard times, and moved away from their rambling mansion to an unpretentious red brick building named Peter's House in a suburb of Bexhill called Sidley.

I had developed an addiction to Barratt's Sherbet Fountains, and had discovered that, if I walked the three miles from Bexhill Station to Sidley after school, the three old pence of bus fare saved would suffice to buy two of those delectable and badly printed yellow cylinders with a tube of liquorice projecting out of the top.

Auntie Honour, the house mother, was puzzled for months why I arrived home late, tired, beautifully happy, and eructating the carbon dioxide gas that sherbet gives off copiously. But this routine was finally responsible for my quitting the moderate centre of British politics, and adopting an attitude somewhat to the right of Vlad the Impaler, at least where law and order are concerned.

One afternoon, three roughly dressed and somewhat older village boys followed me out of Bexhill into the countryside. At first, they merely jostled me from time to time, then tried to stamp on my feet. I plodded on wordlessly, and this annoyed them all the more, so that they began to aim cuffing blows at me, and to try and boot me up the backside.

Outnumbered as I was, and far from home, I put up with their insults for about a mile. They could not know that, although I was smallish, I spent a large part of each day defending myself with a middle-class ferocity that they had probably never encountered.

I waited until the biggest boy – whom I had identified as their leader – got too close, then landed a punch to his agreeably soft solar plexus with my full six and a half stone behind it. He crumpled to the ground, gasping for air like a recently-landed blowfish, and trying to weep at the same time. One of his accomplices shouted, 'Dirty toff, you bloody gorn and killed 'im.'

Quoting Palliser, the reigning school bully at St Giles, I riposted, 'If you can't join them, beat them.'

5

After four terms at St Giles, I was judged to be sufficiently hardened off to go to a boarding prep school. At the time, my father was only earning about £700 a year, and I have often wondered how on earth he managed financially, with two children at private schools, and a way of life in Africa that was not particularly cheap. Admittedly, the fares home were all paid every two-and-a-half years, but the six months of peregrinations that followed must have made a big hole in their slender savings.

Lilian, Ronald and I went down to look over the Junior King's School at Milner Court, near Canterbury. We had heard that its connection with the South African pioneer Lord Milner meant that the sons of white sahibs were especially welcome there.

When we arrived, the granitic head was all engaging smiles and warm reassurance. And his charming wife laughed airily as she fell backwards into the River Stour, while demonstrating to us how the boys were free to canoe up and down that weed-strewn riverlet. Laughing boys, each in an exiguous garment made specially for the school, and baptized by them a bimbag, frolicked shouting round the murky pool, full, as I could see, of freshwater snails, in which I was promised that I would quickly learn to swim.

But when a few weeks later I arrived by train to join their flock, things seemed rather different. A sixteen-stone, six-foot-four battle-scarred survivor of the first Great War, the Head saw boys who did not come up to his high expectations as the sort of deserters, cowards and looters, that in his military days, he would have broken on the wheel. Once for example, early on in my time at his school and during the dreaded meeting known as 'Reports', he started by telling us that we were all getting slack and inefficient, and worked himself into such a frenzy that the old shrapnel wound on his neck stood lividly out.

'You've asked for it,' he concluded suddenly, face working, 'and now I have decided to bring you all to your senses. The whole Upper School will file through the door into the classroom next door, and I will give each boy one stroke of the cane.'

The bespectacled swots in the Sixth Form began a low lamentation at this, but nevertheless lined up to step through the door as ordered. As each one did so, he was immediately hit on the buttocks with a thick cane, brought by an acolyte from the Head's study.

With practice, his speed built up, so that quite soon bottoms were being cracked at almost the firing rate of a Maxim gun. We juniors cowered in our seats as the hair-raising yowlings and blows echoed through the hall, hoping that the Head would not be gripped by crazed bloodlust, change his mind and go for the unique feat of beating the whole school. Afterwards, an older boy who did not escape the charnel house, told me that the Head had a rictus of glee on his face as he went to work.

As I moved through the school, usually in the upper quartile of any particular class, my application and modest achievements seemed only to further his distaste for me. Sometimes I pondered what reasons he could possibly have for being so beastly. For example, I knew that I had offended him one day at lunch. I was sitting near him and, being unfamiliar with English etiquette on the subject, stored the stones from a bowlful of damsons in my cheek until it bulged like a marsupial's pouch.

Finally, the flesh would stretch no more, so I put my lips to the rim of the plate and squeezed them out like toothpaste. When I straightened up, the Head's icy blue stare was on me. Then he said, 'I see that you were brought up by the baboons in Africa, Moreau. We don't like dirty monkey behaviour here.'

I was also very aware that the Mouse Wars made him atrabilious. I took with me to school a beloved white mouse called Eek – occasionally he seemed to be my only real friend. Because there were complaints that he smelt, I was forced to keep his cage further and further away from the classrooms, until he was finally banished to the stable in the tithe barn more than two hundred yards from where I spent my day. Because wild mice and rats in there used to attack him through the wire of his cage, I often took him into classes up my sleeve. This was discovered when a sharp-eyed master saw whiskers and a pink nose agitating out of my cuff. I had to write lines promising not to cause uproar in class by bringing in livestock.

Then the animal-lover mistress who taught one of the bottom classes claimed that my mouse passed his solitary confinement in the barn unfed and unwatered. I told them in vain that he was both a dipsomaniac and a gormandizer, and that I could not shuttle fast enough to and fro to keep his bowls full. She nevertheless set me five hundred more lines, saying, 'I must not torture God's Creatures.' Of course, she told the Head, who took to roaring at me across the school playground as I played 'He', 'Moreau, have you nourished your unfortunate rodent today?'

I tried taking my mouse to bed in the evenings to protect him from things that went bump in the night, but this was quickly discovered when a host of droppings were found under my pillow.

It was clear that I could not win, so, the next term I sadly left poor little Eek at home.

I hoped in vain that this would placate my big enemy, but it didn't. Finally, I discovered what the real trouble was. It was my precocious grasp of the Facts of Life. I found this out one day when, aged about 10, I was giving an impromptu seminar on reproductive physiology in an unoccupied classroom. A small audience of lads of my own age were sitting round in rank incomprehension, occasionally asking questions about their mothers, sisters and pets which usually tailed off into embarrassed sniggers. Suddenly the door burst open. It was my giant persecutor, the Headmaster. He had clearly been listening to my knowall lecturette, and his eyes were blazing. I stood up, white little legs trembling under my grey shorts.

'Damn you,' he shrieked, 'I heard you, shattering their innocence. How can I face their parents, with scum like you preparing them for Broadmoor?' He kicked accurately, his size fourteen brogue hitting my thin bottom so forcefully that my mouth snapped shut, narrowly missing my tongue, and I levitated a foot in the air.

This experience confirmed to me that Mummy had passed on some pretty incendiary information when, aged four and still in Africa, I had asked her where our pet baby Colobus monkey had come from. She had launched into a meticulous biological explanation about sperm and ova, with my father, who in his daily role as Professor Gonad, regarded the whole matter as routine, contributing words like 'gamete' and 'zygote' from the sidelines. Years later, I discovered that he held strong views that no one of any age should be wandering through life uninformed on these basic matters.

It was all the more puzzling to me that the Head had this aversion to talking about human reproduction, because he had six large, healthy children of his own, which indicated to me that he must have had a nodding acquaintance with the acts that produced little Colobus monkeys.

Strangely enough, this friendly concern by my parents that we should not go ignorantly out into the world had rather similar consequences for my sister Prinia. The Gestapo at one of her penitentiaries became aware that she possessed this disgraceful information too, and she was shortly expelled in case she should try to pass it on.

Anyway, the following term, in a pre-emptive strike as I climbed out of the taxi that had brought me from the station, the Head sidled up to me – if men of those intimidating proportions can sidle – and said menacingly, 'Any more of those advanced biology lessons, this term, Moreau, and I shall beat some decency into you.'

He also wrote a letter to the Headmaster of the Senior School where I was supposed to be going next, warning that I was an obsessional sexpot and, if my new Head was temerarious enough to allow me to join his community, I was certain to spread my revolting knowledge through it. Canon Shirley told me, years later, that he reassured his subordinate that, judging by his own impressions of the burgeoning sexuality of his adolescent charges, there was little further that could be done to debauch them. I later discovered how right he was.

Not that everything at the Junior School in Sturry was either

33

tainted by sex or blighted by Headmasterly menace. We had several gangs that provided exciting bouts of warfare. I was a member of the Jones Gang, which specialised in ambushes in the school's extensive grounds. We looked down very much on the gang called the VVT, which stood for Very Vulgar Thing. Their form of saluting one another was to drop their shorts, turn round and moon swiftly. The Jones Gang did not regard them as a serious military unit, although there was no question that their salutes aroused much more public interest than ours did.

Once I was approached by a saturnine lad, who invited me to say something really dirty about the leader of yet another gang, Pugh. I realized immediately that he must be a double agent, so confined myself to what I believed to be an innocuous remark: 'Pugh is a heap of chimpanzee excrement.' I had learned the latter term while toddling after my father in the Amani forest, as he examined the droppings of some elephant visitors. But obviously Pugh took it amiss, because shortly afterwards he hit me at the bottom of the spine with a hockey stick, the prep school equivalent in those days of a good chivving up by the Kray Brothers. Finally, after more covert blows, I had to get the Jones Gang to defeat him in a pitched battle, after which, rather like the Crown of England after the Battle of Bosworth Field, he was tossed into a thorn bush.

One winter's day, during a brief truce with the Head, after a heavy snowfall, he towed me on skis behind a horse. Despite the cannonade of snow clods from the hooves, I loved the feeling so much that I still ski with passion twice a year.

We regularly had lecturers down to entertain us. One was a miniature fellow in shorts and a bush shirt, who wore a huge Bowie knife on his belt. His talk was billed as the story of his walk round the world. He showed a few luridly painted slides of the hot springs at Rotorua and native war canoes in the Solomon Islands (colour photography was not yet fully invented), rapping masterful signals for changes of picture with the blade of his knife on the desk.

Quite soon after his walk started, a gunfight broke out in Chicago. With his face distorted into a brutal mask, he started firing from behind the old upright piano on the left of the stage, mouthing explosive stuttering noises as he began a deadly advance towards the Hymns Ancient and Modern stacked on the far side. Excited screams from his audience so encouraged him that he began circling the lectern at a trot, firing steadily until breath and ammunition ran out.

The same realism was deployed when he was seized by a boa constrictor while walking through the South American jungle. As the huge reptile's slimy coils tightened round him, he clung more and more desperately to the desk (representing a Chita-chita tree), as his face empurpled and veins knotted on his neck. Then, just as his legs began to thrash with a terminal agony, he found his salvation, managing to jerk the trigger of his still-holstered .45 revolver. The shocked boa instantly loosened its grip, and crashed off through the undergrowth. This left our lecturer wan and sagging, but he rallied later, and gave an ataxic re-enactment of a walk that he took through Yokohama during the great earthquake there in 1923, when 180,000 people were killed.

We applauded wildly at the end, as if a half-holiday had been declared, and, rather flattered, our hero presented the boy who had operated the magic lantern with a tiny stuffed alligator.

Some months later, a newspaper reported that this pocket circumnavigator had gone to prison for false pretences, a police sergeant with no sense of romance saying in evidence that it was doubtful if the prisoner had ever walked further than Bexley-heath.

The school also owned eight horses and ponies, which represented varying degrees of threat to life and limb. Smoky, for example, a completely black Dartmoor pony, would begin bucking violently from the moment of being mounted, leaping in the air with his legs held stiffly out, so as to make his landing as brain-shaking as possible. A few really good riders among us seemed to enjoy this, like Western cowboys in a bronco-busting competition. But, after Smoky threw me during a point-to-point in the school grounds and I was carried semiconscious to the sanatorium, and another horse called Belliver turned its double-jointed neck and bit me on the right knee when I pulled on its right rein, I decided that I was not brave enough to be an equestrian. Nevertheless, up to the point where riding really began to hurt, I remember with some nostalgia the flashing gallops over dew-soaked grass in the early mornings, and the tank-like pleasure of crashing at speed through the damp undergrowth of the Sturry woods.

Already by 1938, we became very aware of the rumours of war. When the great silver cigar of the Graf Zeppelin hovered over us, a dozen hands shot up to point gun-like at it, amid explosive mouth noises. And, at the military display at nearby Manston in June, a flight of three Hawker Hurricanes – a substantial percentage of the RAF's total inventory at the time – swooped about in group aerobatics, then curved in to land and stand in a gleaming static display for us to admire.

We noted the four .303 machine guns poking out of the leading edge of each wing, and excitedly pitied the adversary who faced that firepower.

A few days later, a Hurricane caught fire in the air over the school, and we watched the silver canopy of the pilot's parachute blossom as he fell towards the trees not a mile away. The luckier boys piled into a master's car to race over and succour the shaken airman.

We all felt proud to hear of Squadron Leader MacLachan's extraordinary flight in another Hurricane, from Edinburgh to Northolt in forty-five minutes, with a violent tailwind. It seemed to us that in any forthcoming conflict we would be invincible.

6

After the usual crises of kleptomania at age ten, and hyper-genitalism at age ten and a half, I fell into what I believe Kraft-Ebbing called a 'profound Horatian *nil admirare*', marvelling at nothing.

I had tried riding, and it had given me up. I had been sworn into the Jones gang, endured initiation rituals that made the Masai ones look brief and considerate, then been cashiered after a short court martial for failing to turn up to an ambush.

A recruiting office had tried to get me to join the VVT, but it was winter, and I decided that I might get a chill if I mooned constantly in such weather – Kent was always colder than anywhere else in England.

No, it seemed increasingly clear to me that life only held two further excitements: actually dying in some spectacular and terrible way, or watching a grown-up having his appendix out.

Of course, like my contemporaries, I derived what enter-tainment I could from the eccentric antics of the staff, who, in those days often behaved in ways that might get them sent to the psychiatrist nowadays. Some just made bad jokes, like the geometry master who always named the corners of his triangles P, Q and R, so that he could say: 'Now, this is a rather PECULIAR problem'; the geography master who, having said that the sea bed was covered in primeval ooze, then demanded, 'And 'oose responsible for it?'; and the French master who told the same witticism most periods: 'Why do the French call a librarian *un bibliothecaire*?' Answer: 'Because he *tecare* of the *bibliothèque*.' But the two masters who came nearest to helping me forget my death wish were Mr Knatchbull Price, whose left buttock had been blown away at Loos and replaced by moulded cork, which acted as a kind of primitive barometer by squeaking when prolonged dry spells were on the way; and Mr Kenworthy, who always claimed that his withered right hand had been caused by an enraged hippopotamus stepping on it during a point to point outside Nairobi.

Kenworthy always took out the school rides, and perhaps it was his own experience with the hippopotamus that enabled him to remain massively indifferent to the frequent blubbering that went on when it was excessively cold, or we were tossed out of the saddle into beds of nettles by Smoky. He also had a horrible little Jack Russell called Giles, which bit everybody, and showed no sense of humour at all when we tried to put paper hats on him, or sticky notices reading: *Danger: Leg at Half Cock*.

But Kenworthy had recently left the school, taking with him one of the matrons with whom there had been torrid goings on, all the more interesting because most of us thought that she was turning into a man. So we had managed for some months, wringing what entertainment we could out of the Knatch-buttock and the black comedy of the Headmaster. When the latter was not indulging in what used to be called 'Fright-fulness' in the first Great War, he could occasionally be risible when suddenly on Active Service again – as long as he didn't see you smirking, because then retribution was liable to be swift and terrible.

One worthwhile occasion for the rest of us was when Jupp II got his big ginger head jammed in a nightpot while attitudinis-ing as a German soldier. Another was when Lumsden got stuck in the tallest poplar tree, and had to be rescued by a military-style operation involving improvised sheerlegs, a line hurled aloft with weight on the end, and a bosun's chair, and lots of shouted orders.

Then Mr Burtley joined the staff, and in the twinkling of an eye all was changed. He began his career as No 1 entertainer with a bang. Most prep school masters seem to need a running in period before they give vent to the full range of their eccentricities, but not so Burtley. From Day One, he pulled out all the stops.

He was a vulturine, stooping figure with luminous white curls, and all visible skin surfaces the colour of boiled silverside. We watched spellbound as, several times in the very first Latin class, a tremor began in his left hand, slowly augmenting, until finally the whole arm was lashing about like a recently-landed conger eel. Smiling reposefully, as if he had only now noticed that there was trouble at the periphery, Burtley stilled it with a friendly grip from his other hand.

Then he began shooting thundery glances over his shoulder, muttering angrily, and finally slamming a violent backhander into the space behind his chair, rumbling, 'Hornets, hornets, hornets!'

On other days, he would shut one eye, and conduct the whole class with only the other one open, or start doing gruesome little conjuring tricks on his person, such as seeming to saw off his thumb with a penknife, lifting the pale looking severed part up for inspection. Or he would push a gorily bedizened nail through the palm of his hand, grunting with the effort of working it through.

As with the Head, it was inadvisable to show that you had noticed anything out of the ordinary going on, let alone to laugh. Once, when Mr Burtley was marking an exercise with his red pen held between his teeth, a boy at the back tittered. Shouting furiously, Burtley hurled his pocketful of change at the tasteless offender.

'That's the way that shellshock takes you,' opined an eleven-year-old wiseacre during break afterwards, 'I had an uncle who got it on the Somme, and afterwards he used to stand up in church and shout at the Vicar during the sermon.' It was common knowledge that Burtley had been a sniper in the Artists' Rifle during the first Great War, and that he had been badly wounded and decorated.

We all agreed that it would while away morning prayers much faster if Burtley could be induced to interrupt the Chaplain in the same way.

He also had mysterious turns of phrase. If you were showing signs of dimness in answering questions in class, for example, he would exclaim, 'Why, a child of two with a wooden leg would know that.'

For my eleventh birthday, (God, I was nearly into my teens, and soon I would have to brush my hair and do my teeth every day so that, as Aunt Lilian frequently said, one day some misguided girl wouldn't find me too revolting), I was given an autograph book. After ensuring that I occupied the most desirable place in it by writing in minuscule with a mapping pen on the bottom millimetre of the last page: 'By hook or by crook, I'll be last in this book', I took it to my new hero Burtley.

With a great deal of muttering cogitation, Burtley selected an eau-de-nil coloured page, peered at it closely for imperfections, then drew a gibbon-like hominoid with a stubbly chin and lovable round eyes, pencilling underneath 'A Burtiwit'. This still seemed not quite to satisfy him, and he sat frowning and humming *Roses of Picardy* to himself for a few moments, before adding neatly below in Latin: *Hercules, in hora una, septem feminis satisfacere potuit.* Meaning, as I later learned, 'Hercules, in a single hour, could bring seven women to ecstasy.'

With a flourish, he signed it 'Cassivelaunus Wilhelm Musgrave Burtley,' saying, rightly as it proved, 'This will remind you, Kennedy, that *satisfacere* takes the dative. Doubtless also, in after years, when your Latin improves, it will be a source of wonder.'

He often pretended to mistake me for one of the cross-eyed, bedwetting Kennedy brothers, just as there was a whole segment of the school that he called Apps in honour of another boy, who was going bald by the unusual route of pulling out his head hairs one by one.

Every Christmas, as part of the mostly grim rituals before we broke up, the staff used to put on a shadow pantomime from behind a line of sheets hung between the pillars on the stage of the dining hall which screened them from the audience of boys. Looking back, although it all seemed quite Victorian at the time, in fact the actors were probably hugging themselves – and for all I know, one another, since plenty of ladies were involved – at the complex double meanings that they managed to slip in.

Anyway, at his first Yuletide, Burtley was supposed to shoot a small bird, hopping about in a branch held aloft by the Headmaster, while twittering bird noises were made in the background by the rather gipsy-looking lady who taught the tots in the bottom class.

As the huge, eerie shadow of Cassivelaunus Burtley advanced on his lovably tweeting prey, we could see that he was pointing his own .410 shotgun.

Stalking across the stage, he intoned in his lugubrious basso:

'There was a little man,
Who had a little gun,
His bullets were made of liquorice.
He shot some great big crows,
Right through the parson's nose,
And the bullets came out at the vicarage.'

So saying, he raised his shadowy gun. There was a flash and a tremendous bang, followed by the sound of plaster, the branch and the wreckage of the mechanical bird, all making crash landings.

'Damn you, Burtley,' we all heard the deafened Headmaster scream, standing as he was in front of a stage side pillar, which now had a gaping crater in it no more than fifteen inches above his massive head.

The show ended abruptly and we all trooped out, speculating excitedly whether the ex-sniper had really meant to frighten the wits out of his boss, or whether leaving a round up the breech was just the kind of absentmindedness to be expected of a shellshock victim.

Anyway, the result of this debacle was that the Head's eyes would narrow whenever he saw Burtley about the place with a gun under his arm. This was very frequently, because he was the school's Armaments Officer, and taught shooting with a fair degree of eccentricity on the range that we had in the roof of one of the school's wings.

One of the school's most Victorian tenets was that, if we were rooted out of bed early enough, sent on an early morning run, then forced to have cold showers, this would stop us playing with ourselves as puberty neared. If our bowels could be kept wide open as well with well-aimed cascara, this would further reduce the incidence of onanism.

There was one other compensation now that Burtley had arrived. As we panted past the Master's cottage on our icy morning run, we would sometimes hear the strong ex-soldier's voice in the bath, raised in the sort of song that few prep schools echo to – about a warm-hearted street girl called Lily, who plied her trade in Piccadilly, while her mother performed a similar service in the Strand; or another one about a singularly well-equipped ram in Derbyshire, and what his amazing delivery system enabled him to do socially, before three men and an omnibus had to transport it sorrowfully for burial in St Paul's.

When the summer came, Burtley proved to be a marvellous googly bowler. Up to the wicket he would pad, like some bent-kneed predator, and dance one joking step. Then with a flash of boiled silverside, the ball would swerve towards the batsman, whirring with spin.

In the Fathers' Match that year, he came into his own. By the time it arrived, most of the fathers had heard about Burtley over the Easter holiday breakfast tables, and there were rumours of parental hints to the already half-convinced Head that Burtley was Not Quite Nice.

When the day arrived, the fathers came in to bat one by one, office-pale, plump-handed, with motheaten hairlines, and unleashed good-natured cowshots to save their sons from public shame. Burtley's googlies wove their way round a series of feebly wagging bats, and wicket after wicket crashed.

Trugg-Lee's hairy, thick-waisted Dad came in sixth. He was the hero of these occasions, shop steward of the fathers, and always the first to protest.

'Can't let that potty blighter get away with it,' he blared, as he strode out from the pavilion. Bounding out of the crease, he lashed the first ball for a four, letting out a bray of unkind stockbroker's laughter at the bowler. Burtley began his next run up. He went a little faster than usual, and, as his hand blurred over, he bellowed, 'No ball!' His hand was empty. The ball was in his pocket. Trugg-Lee had danced over the popping crease, ready for a tremendous swipe. Some buffoonery was expected on these occasions, and, as he ran back to his wicket, Trugg-Lee tried to look as if he was enjoying it.

He took his stance again. This time, Burtley pounded up from double his usual distance. His arm hurtled over and, as Trugg-Lee ducked frantically, the ball whined by in a flat trajectory, to smack into the sight screen, dozens of yards behind.

'Steady on, Burtley,' said the Head with his well-known

cold-eyed look, no doubt remembering the bird shot which had so nearly parted his hair.

'*Homo sum, humani nil a me alienum puto,*' rumbled back Burtley conversationally. The fathers within earshot shook their heads.

Last ball of the over. A Newbolt-like hush. Up came Burtley, arms flailing. Crouched in grim expectation, Trugg-Lee backed a yard. Everybody had seen the ball in his right hand as he ran up, but it wasn't there now. Then, as he braked to a standstill, a trickling underarm came from his other hand.

Caught off his guard, Trugg-Lee let it bounce three times before he scythed round at it, forgetting that he was standing alongside his stumps. Satisfyingly, his bat smashed backwards into them.

'No ball,' thundered Burtley, dancing a small sniper's jig with delight. Trugg-Lee was safe that time, but his nerve had gone, and he fell to an ordinary spinner in the next over. I took a long pull on my sherbet fountain. There would be no *nil admirari* during the weeks that it would take Trugg-Lee and Burtley to sort this one out.

7

Accustomed by now to our world falling to pieces round us at regular intervals, Prinia and I could only muster one or two perfunctory tears when, one day in 1938, our foster parents announced that they were also leaving the country and going back to Egypt. Ronald was to be a full colonel there, and run a whole Army department. Lilian would be doing something that she did very well – arranging elegant social events as a gracious hostess.

Our new guardians were to be a couple called Watson, who lived with their three children in Rochester. They had a terrace house on high ground, not far from the River Medway. Mr Watson, a muscular, cauliflower-eared ex-Rugby player, seemed to take an instant dislike to me, which he masked as best he could over the succeeding year.

His wife, prematurely snow white like Lilian, was very kind and tried to make us welcome. Their solidly-built daughter Ann was unremarkable in most respects, except that, later on, when doing a Cambridge entrance exam aged about seventeen, she somehow contrived to marry one of her middle-aged invigilators. The Watsons also had a baby of about five, who was in the process of being spoilt rotten.

Christopher, their son, destined to become a doctor, was of an adventurous turn of mind. Together, we used to explore the malodorous miles of tunnels in the abandoned fortifications that ran along the Medway, which had once protected the naval base at Chatham. They were left over from Napoleonic times, and we always dreamed of finding a rusty iron bound box full of doubloons in a dark corner. In fact, all that I ever found was a William IV penny and the battered remains of a church-warden's pipe.

A younger boy called Cyril often came with us, to hold the spare matches and candles, and generally to act as an acolyte.

Because we were older, he was always very respectful, and, as part of the process of subjugation, I ordered him to address us only in Latin, of which I now had a smattering, particularly the Principal Parts of defective verbs, and bad jokes from Burtley, such as '*Malo*, I would rather be, *malo*, up an apple tree.'

Classics had not yet started for Cyril, so we taught him enough pidgin Latin to be able to communicate. I then refused to answer unless he addressed me as *Davidibus*, and, in his role of porter and *cisibeo*, he had to refer to his waxy charges as *candelibuses*. The whole effect was heightened by the fact that he had both a stammer and a lisp, so that, as we marched resolutely through the dark, dripping mazes, there would be breathless shouts from fifty yards behind of, *Davidibuth, mith can-can-candelibutheth extinctati th-th-thunt. Nihil video.*' In the same idiom, he was supposed to call Christopher *Atrebates*, but he generally forgot, and his various speech impediments spoiled the rolling euphony of the name, and he could not usually get past the A-A-A-A- anyway.

At that time, too, Christopher and I discovered a pheno- menon which had agreeable elements of the supernatural about it. Watching the Short Brothers pickaback seaplane Mercury taxiing in the Medway to be hoist aboard its mother aircraft Maia – Mercury was later to set a record for the non-stop flight to South Africa that has never been beaten – we ventured out on to the glutinous, dark green river mud. This had all the untrustworthy properties of quicksand, and we sank rapidly up to our knees and beyond if we stood still. But, if we adopted a loping, weightless gait in our gumboots, we could tittup across the ooze like huge sandpipers, pursued by satisfying shouted warnings from the bank that we were about to disappear for ever.

The combined families often used to travel to a big roller skating rink at Gillingham, where we would race round a wooden floor to the accompaniment of booming music. When I had achieved my dream of a pair of skates with ball bearings to diminish effort, I then yearned for a pair with wide rubber composite wheels that I saw being used by experts at the rink to reach unimaginable speeds.

The Munich crisis of 1938 burst upon us. With hindsight it

45

seems that by this time Herr Hitler had ceased to be just a human being, and had become a force of nature. When Lloyd George went and fawned on him at the Adlers Horst, Eden delightedly exchanged reminiscences of the Somme with him, and, finally, Chamberlain nodded assent over the entrails of Czechoslovakia, it seemed the same magnetism that he projected, silently staring like Svengali at his audience before making a speech, had enthralled our leaders as well. But, as mere children, we thought that everything that our Government did must automatically be right. And in any case, given our state of unreadiness, it is hard to see what the alternative was.

Watson supervised Christopher and myself as we dug through his vegetable patch to a depth of eight feet, then roofed the dank, loamy hole that resulted with neat hessian sandbags, propped up on pieces of 4 × 4 timber. By primitive trigonometry, we had calculated how far the house at the end of the garden would fall when bombed, and sited our dugout so as to ensure our survival when it happened.

Chamberlain appeared back at the airport after stabbing an ancient democracy in the back, and war fever died. The dugout began to be the haunt of toads, grass snakes and long, etiolated nettles.

The relationship with the Watsons limped on, until I began to wonder whether the father had got wind of the facts of life brouhaha at my school, and was afraid that I would begin holiday seminars. This occurred to me particularly when, on a trip out in the family's asthmatic Morris 12, we went through a leafy Kent village called Borstal, and Watson said meaningfully, 'This is where you might well end up, David, if you're not very careful.'

Then my parents arrived back from Africa and rescued us for a six months break. My father had the habit of buying patrician limousines for a few pounds when he came home on leave, selling them a few months later for a similar price. On this occasion, he bought an immense six-seater Armstrong Siddeley for £25, complete with a cocktail cabinet, cigarette lighters and pop-up vanity mirrors in the back for the titled former owners to admire themselves before stepping out to greet their serfs.

Behind our electrically operated glass screen, we played with these accoutrements endlessly on the long journeys.

In this heroic vehicle, we sped out to Pembrokeshire in western Wales, to stay in a rambling, tumbledown farmhouse on the coast near the tiny port of Solva. Along this blessed, empty coastline, where you could see for miles in the smokeless air, we ran and tumbled about on the endless sandy beaches, and explored the rich life of the rock pools, while my mother directed the collection of the yellow horned poppy, samphire and sea rocket from the cliffs.

It happened to be harvest time, and we were all happy to stook the corn, load it on to carts, and build big ricks in the corners of the fields. I often rode on the corn cutting and binding machine behind the tractor. It threw neat sheaves out at one side, tied round the middle with hemp, while the blades chattered through the undergrowth of the cornfield on the other. On a good day, hares and rabbits would race out of the diminishing shelter that was left to them in the middle of the field, and dogs and humans would pant after them, knowing that weeks of good stews depended on their fleetness.

The family also had a wild young relative who lived from trapping rabbits on their rolling, overgrown five hundred acres, and selling them to the local butcher. I used to go round with him in his cart as he set his hundreds of traps. Even in those days, it seemed to me a shame to kill such pretty animals in such an ugly way. He and I could not argue about it, because he only really spoke Welsh. But, by the end of the holiday I could manage nearly as much in his lilting language as I could in Swahili.

The farm's water supply came from a nearby pond, in the bottom of which a hydraulic ram thumped as it pumped the water up into the tank in the roof. Using the water's own pressure to power it thirty feet into the air seemed to me miraculous, and I have been looking ever since for someone who can tell me how this perpetual motion is achieved.

In the freemasonry of the bird world, my father had come to know R. M. Lockley, famous as the author of books such as *I Know an Island*, and for his lifelong hobby of running remote bird sanctuaries. He had recently taken over one of the wild

47

islands off the Pembroke coast called Skokholm, which sits in the sea a few miles from the cliffs of the much bigger Ramsey Island, and the uninhabited gannet sanctuary of Grassholm.

One day, my father hired a long motor fishing boat from Dale, round the coast to the south, and we crossed the rough sound to the primitive landing stage on Lockley's island. It was an unforgettable day on the hundred or so acres high above the plunging ocean, surprising puffins in their burrows, watching the black backed gulls wrestling with one another, and seeing the giant gannets legging it along the cliffs for take-off.

My parents, whenever they had the opportunity of voting in British elections, always chose diametrically opposed candidates. Thus, my mother would solemnly vote Conservative, while my father voted Labour, so that they neatly cancelled one another out. They followed a similar policy in religion. As a vicar's daughter, my mother had acquired the lifelong habit of communing regularly with God. My father made gentle fun of her beliefs, and went off in the opposite direction.

Thus it was that, on September 3rd, 1939, he went for a characteristically agnostic bird walk, while my mother, sister and I filed into the ancient dark red cathedral at St David's, to sit on the uncomfortable chairs in the nave for Matins. By a miracle of technology, the Bishop had contrived to get Mr Chamberlain on the public address system of the pulpit, and at 11 o'clock precisely we heard him in his sonorous Victorian voice declare war on Germany. There was a memorable gasp from the congregation.

Afterwards, the whole family went down to a nearby beach. Prinia and I were half-hoping to hear the desynchronised throbbing of Nazi engines overhead as we animatedly discussed what this new state of affairs might mean to us. There would be deaths, we knew, and a lot of destruction, with heroic deeds galore. Perhaps our parents would be trapped in the U.K. as well, and we would remain a complete and normal family again, like our friends at school.

We had already been issued with the ugly but effective civilian gas masks, and we imagined that we might spend days gasping through them in choking clouds of the gas that *Picture Post* said was a distinct possibility. Anderson shelters were sprouting in every garden and some really smart people had taken delivery of a wonderful new shelter which was made of steel thick enough to withstand the weight of your collapsing house, but pending this event stood in your dining room in lieu of the ordinary table. It was thought that many lives would be saved by the ability to scramble into its safety even when you were eating, at the first sound of whistling missiles descending. Our excited forebodings were given more substance when, as we walked back off the golden sand, the first sirens began to howl.

When we got back to our ancient Welsh farm, the head of the house had shown that, when his family and friends seemed to be under threat, he had dramatically effective reflexes. As the National Anthem was dying away after Chamberlain's speech, he had jumped in his old car and raced to the nearest town of Haverfordwest. There, he had gone round one grocer after another until the back seat of his car was full of all the items that he thought would get short if food was rationed. He brought back stones of sugar, twenty pounds of butter, armfuls of flour, and more cheese than I had ever seen at once. Years later he told me that his prescience had given them all a tremendous diet right through the war. But a few days after he did it, this sort of behaviour was condemned as anti-social hoarding and black marketeering.

8

Since Rochester was barely twenty minutes' flying time from the Continent for a well-tuned Messerschmitt, our parents did not send us back there. Instead, they made an arrangement with a Miss Olive Jeans, who ran a guest house 700 feet up on the chalk downs two miles outside Marlborough, in Wiltshire. Middle-aged, unmarried and very religious, she owned Granham House, a beautiful twelve-bedroom structure built in 1788, and with splendid views across chalky downland to Savernake Forest several miles away.

Hitherto her clientele had been elderly schoolmasters, civil servants and minor dons, most of whom appreciated the uneventful way of life, home cooking and long country walks that were possible. But, with the tide of evacuees from 1939 on, all this had changed.

For one thing, the City of London School was evacuated to join Marlborough College, and a dozen boys and masters were billeted on us. Then there was food rationing. When my sister and I were on holiday, it was part of our war work to hurtle down the massive Granham Hill into the town astride our ancient, rusty bicycles – mine had cost ten shillings – to buy formidable amounts of provender. With thirty or more people munching away in the house, our return journey uphill was a feat, wheeling meat rations, butter, margarine, fruit and everything else on our rickety machines.

Washing up was also part of our duties. Often, it lasted several hours a day. Prinia busied herself with general house-work too, and I did heavy gardening, mainly carving up hedges, digging for victory and axeing down trees in the couple of acres that surrounded the house.

We nourished and milked the nanny goat as well, and because Granham had no electricity, we saw that everyone had

50

candles in their rooms, cleaned smoky lamp chimneys, trimmed wicks, and poured in the scarce paraffin.

Not that our lives were in the least joyless. For example, one bright wartime morning, my sister was performing the kermats of a Greek dance, barefoot across the dewy lawn. Suddenly, from the direction of the ancient green-painted earth closet, hidden in a yew arbour, came the crack of an air rifle. I had magnanimously lent my beloved .177 calibre Daisy, complete with a box of slugs, to the sixteen-year-old Hutchinson, partly because I knew that he fancied my sister, and I felt encouraging.

But it had not occurred to me that his idea of a love ploy would be to shoot her in the right calf muscle as she cavorted about – rather a creditable shot on a moving target, really. Fortunately, at that time I had a fantasy that I might one day earn my living by wielding a scalpel, so I was glad to pull out my multi-purpose Pocket Scout's Tool, complete with tiny chromium plated axe, and winkle out the deformed little slug with a sharp device intended, I believe, for gralloching salmon. Shortly, a contrite Hutchinson left his sniper's post at the window of the malodorous privy, and he came sheepishly out to act as a medical auxiliary.

That was not the only time that this redoubtable girl came under fire. Once we were having a game of William Tell in the same part of the garden, and, playing the name part, I was twice ordered by the brutal Landvocht Gessler to shoot her high-crowned velour school hat off her head.

The bullets made neat entry holes on one side, and trap flaps for their exit holes on the other. We healed these honourable wounds with sticking plaster on the inside, and, before going back to her fee-paying Borstal in Reading, she concealed them further by arranging a sort of pork pie effect, like the racy style worn at the time by lounge lizards along with suede shoes and camel hair coats.

On the first church parade of the term, the Sergeant Majoress who led it ordered my sister to restore her hat to its customary towering, St Trinian's shape, thus exposing the slug punctures. Thinking what a good bit of news it would make to report in the extravagant letters we regularly wrote to one another, she

51

thought of explaining that she had been shot in the hat when caught in the open during the hols by a strafing Stuka bomber, but finally opted for saying that our Wiltshire retreat abounded in gigantic clothes moths which practically machine-gunned her wardrobe.

She was not, however, the only casualty from rifle fire in the hillside garden. I myself, on another of the occasions when I was overcome with a foolish desire to be liked by my evacuee contemporaries, had lent my air rifle to a madcap refugee called Jurg. From a commanding position in a tree, he shot away my morning bowl of porridge from the summerhouse table in front of me. A sliver of the pellet lodged in the cornea of my right eye.

Fascinated as I was by the honourably wounded soldiery who circulated in the area in bright blue suits and red ties, I took the opportunity to identify with this group by tying a mock-bloodstained field dressing round my head and over the eye concerned.

With difficulty, I was persuaded to take off this badge of honour in order to carry out my Sunday duty of reading the lesson in my piping treble in Clench Common church. Tears streamed down my face as I made my way haltingly through Ecclesiastes. Afterwards, a good farmer's wife, appropriately called Mrs Bullock – who always wore a black wickerwork hat pulled down over her eyes and ears, and had no roof to her mouth – asked me if I had a stye in my eye.

'No, Mrs Bullock, actually I was sort of shot in the eye yesterday,' I said proudly.

'Poor lad,' she said kindly, addressing her fellow parishioners after the service, 'E's go' a li'le homehing in 'is eye from a bulle'.'

When I come to think of it, lead was always flying around the place, to remind us of the English Army's inching progress across the sandy African wastes.

Once, the Vicar of Pewsey's wife was in the hallway, chatting agreeably about the fine crop of quinces that we had enjoyed in that summer of '42. My sister and I were standing in direct line down in the orchard, busying ourselves with the nanny goat, which we were about to milk. Suddenly a rifle cracked down on the old railway line 300 yards below. I was thrilled to hear a bullet go *zzmm* between us. It continued its trajectory, to miss the vicar's wife by a hairsbreadth, and bury itself in the panelling of the hall.

'Dear, dear,' she murmured, and went on with her business.

Thinking romantically that it was really my name that had been on the bullet, rather than Mrs Prideaux's, for the next few days I astonished the goat by crawling round her on my hands and knees, keeping her rumbling milk-producing organs between me and the unidentified sniper. Eventually, it became clear that he had gone for easier targets, and I was reassured enough to approach her in a series of darting runs, keeping a wary eye out for tell-tale puffs of smoke from the embankment below in case I had to flatten myself in the goat droppings.

The war was always in the background. From the lawn, we could watch the London barrage every night for months, punctuated occasionally by a huge flash as a land mine went off. And, on particularly exciting nights just before the invasion, we could hear in the otherwise sleepy darkness the rumble of tanks, Bren gun carriers and Bedford lorries in the fields round the garden. In the morning, a small town of khaki-clad strangers would be there, peacefully filling their machines from green five-gallon petrol tins, breaking open powdery-looking K Rations, and whistling after everything female that passed within a hundred yards, including the nanny goat.

The saintly woman who ran Granham had hung a Scripture text in every room except the lavatory, where there was only a notice asking guests not to risk the integrity of the drain by putting unfriendly objects down.

She also played the harmonium in the same little church where I had wept over the lesson. It was unfortunate that the church mice, on short commons like the rest of us, had made do with the leather bellows of the instrument as iron rations. The only person who could have mended them was the local cobbler, and he had been drafted to India on military service. So she had to pedal like a competitor in the Tour de France, and would end a long hymn slumped over the keyboard and panting as if she had just done the hillclimb up Mount Ventoux.

Being so holy, she saw nothing wrong in the tired, pale-faced London women, married to absent Servicemen, who came down for short stays in rooms adjoining what I now recognise as bespectacled, grey haired old rams in reserved occupations.

The backstairs staff that waited on the legitimate and otherwise occupants of the twelve bedrooms consisted of a dashing, ex-postmistress with a Brummy accent, who rode a racing bicycle and was known to us all as Savoury Pud; and a nice-natured eccentric called Billy, who had been let out of a mental institution as harmless when the proprietress requested this cheap labour. One of his eyes seemed to have burrowed under the bridge of his nose on its way to rendezvous with the other, and he bared a set of yellowing fangs nearly an inch long in order to express any emotion. But, in fact, like many of the mentally handicapped, he was really very bright in some areas, and could, for example, expertly mend broken watches.

As a gardener, he suffered from a curious little disability. 'Edges' to him meant what everybody else called 'hedges', and 'hedges' meant the edges of the lawn which needed constant attention because of our endless bicycling on it. Thus, whichever he was asked to do, he was always found later working on the other. Eventually, in despair, the lady of the house adopted his dialect as well when telling him what to do, and then she had no further trouble.

There was also a wild gipsy charwoman called Winnie, who came rather irregularly because, it was rumoured, she was often busy comforting the troops who swarmed in the area.

Occasionally, the guests were of above average interest. T. E. Lawrence's eldest brother, who had spent half a lifetime as a medical missionary in China, stayed for months with his robust, log-sawing mother who was then approaching her century, apparently as strong as the day that she began bearing Sir Thomas Chapman his five sons.

Doctor Lawrence had the disconcerting habit of hissing through his teeth in the self-deprecating Chinese manner when you came into the room where he was. He also had a most eighteenth-century concept of medicine. Called up one day to the room of an elderly aristocrat called Lady Fowler, he prescribed hot antiphlogiston poultices on both ankles. Eventually, we got supplies from the local vet, who had only heard of this strange white porridge being used on the strained cannon bones of thoroughbreds. And I remember Lawrence one day telling the spellbound dining room why it was that birds' eggs had a smaller diameter at one end than the other. It was a marvellous provision of Nature and the Good Lord to ensure that when the eggs rolled to the edge of the nest, the eccentric shape ensured that they rotated back safely to the middle again.

Other guests were Ras Desta and a largish group of the Abyssinian Royal Family. In those days, the security industry had not been properly invented, and the boys moved easily and unrecognized about wartime Wiltshire looking exactly like miniature, unbearded versions of the Lion of Judah.

Miss Batty, a headmistress from somewhere in Scotland where obviously they had little sense of the absurd, was only remarkable because a fellow evacuee managed to set fire to the back folds of her kilt so that she sat pontificating in front of the log fire, while smoke wreathed up behind her from the fine clan wool that clothed her massive backside.

Although it was not officially a temperance hotel, the only strong drink really encouraged was Communion wine on ecclesiatical occasions. One of the grown-up residents, however, kept a quart bottle of sweet vermouth hidden in his potty cupboard. Rummaging through his effects while he was out, one of our evacuee intelligence agents found it, and siphoned off a quantity into a hastily-emptied TCP bottle, which he then used as a hip flask. We all swigged from it on particularly stressful occasions, and this probably accounts for my preference to this day for a slight, halogenated tang in my sweet vermouth.

One night, war abruptly came in earnest to Granham. I had been lying in bed in the summerhouse – my room inside was needed as usual for fee-paying refugees from the Smoke – when I heard the desynchronized throbbing of what I knew was a Heinkel. It seemed to be moving purposefully towards the huge ammunition dump in Savernake Forest, and I imagined that if the pilot let go his bomb load at the right moment, the thatched structure in which we were sleeping would collapse on top of us in the firestorm that would follow.

Then a nightfighter appeared, and there was an exchange of

tracer. The several schoolboys also sleeping in the frail shelter craned excitedly to see what would happen next.

An engine seemed to be enveloped in a ruddy glow, and the plane was losing height. For years I had waited for this moment. Beside me lay the trusty weapon that had shown itself so effective in demolishing bowls of porridge, girlish calves and St Trinian hats.

'Who's coming with me to arrest the German pilot?' I said. There was a stentorian silence. One boy, I know, being a townie, confused wolves and foxes, and never went anywhere at night in the country in case his bones were found gnawed by these vulpines. Now another gave voice to his night terrors.

'There's adders out there,' he said, his voice trembling with fear, 'adders always come out to bite in the dark.'

'Okay,' I said manfully, 'someone has to do these dangerous things.' If I had remembered, I might have quoted Captain Oates, and said, 'I'm just going out. I may be some time.'

Anyway, I pulled on a pair of Billy's old gumboots, and wrapped the motheaten A.R.P. trench coat that did as my dressing gown round my shoulders. Putting the Daisy air gun under my arm, I strode off into the blackness for the two mile walk up to the Forest.

I had my part perfectly rehearsed. First, when you saw dim figures running for cover in the gloom, you shouted as gruffly as you could, '*Halt, oder ich schiesse sofort!*' Then, as they turned slowly to face you, you screamed, '*Hände hoch!*' Then, as they approached their captor fearfully, you ordered, '*Waffen hinlegen. Kommen Sie mit mir an die Polizei.*' The preposition '*an*' was one of those tiresome ones that took an accusative of motion and a dative of place.

As I ran along the cart track to the scene of the action, I tried out these masterly orders on the bunnies that leaped about everywhere in those days before myxomatosis. Somewhere ahead of me now, a large fire seemed to be burning in the darkness. That would be the crash site, where the bewildered – and probably wounded – crew of the bomber would be milling round awaiting a linguistically gifted saviour who could rescue them from the pitchforks of the brutish yokels.

I puffed into the last huge, dark field before the forest. The blaze lay ahead of me. It could only be the wreckage of the Heinkel. There was nothing else in the field to burn. Then I saw figures moving dimly round it.

'*Halt, oder ich schiesse!*' I shrieked, following this immediately with a ringing '*Hände hoch!*', adding with indecent haste, '*Die Polizei erwartet Sie!*'

One of the figures moved away from the fire and came towards me. Far from having his hands in the air, he was clutching a purposeful-looking Lee Enfield rifle.

'Wot was that you said, sonny?' he asked menacingly. 'Are you a Fifth Columnist or sunnig?'

'N-N-No,' I stuttered back, 'I thought a Heinkel had crashed here, and I came to arrest the crew.'

'Oh yeah?' he said mockingly. 'Wiv yer popgun, I s'pose. Well, 'e was after our decoy fire 'ere, but the Beaufighter got 'im before 'e could put it out fer us. I reckon 'e crashed a good five miles away.'

I turned silently, at first disappointed to manly tears as I stumbled back the long way to my bed in the summerhouse. But, by the time that I got there, I had such a bloodcurdling tale to tell that one boy in our outside dormitory had to take refuge in the house, moaning and gibbering with fear. I had told him that every rustle in the darkness outside was the Nazi aircrew coming to make him into soap and lampshades.

9

At school at this time, exciting and warlike things were also happening. The centre block of the E-shaped building was strengthened with blast walls, so that we could remain cowering safely in the smelly changing rooms for anything but a direct hit. Sticky paper was pasted by the hundreds of yards on the large windows to stop glass splinters from whizzing about untidily. Sandbags appeared at strategic points, such as round the entrance to the Headmaster's study. And we were made to don our curiously pig-like civilian masks at regular gas drills.

Then, suddenly, as the Messerschmitt cohorts began to trace their fluffy contrails across the Kent skies in serious numbers, and their much-prized 20 millimetre cannon shell empties began to hail down on the playing fields, the decision was taken to scarper away to Cornwall.

During the fortnight that it took to pack the school up for its three hundred mile journey, we were all sent home. Because I had no real place to go, I was taken in along with his son by a charming GP called Johnson in the quaint Kentish town of Smarden. This man earned my undying respect one day when we were driving in the steep main street of the town. Although he had a bad limp from the first Great War – the result of getting twelve machine gun bullets in the leg while flying in the RFC – he braked sharply and jumped out of his car as we climbed the hill. A drayhorse was bolting in the opposite direction, gathering speed. Somehow, Dr Johnson not only caught up with it, but fought it to a halt before it reached the crowded pavements further down. He got back into the car and drove on before anyone except the terrified driver could thank him. 'I'd like to be an understated hero like that when I grow up,' I thought to myself.

The King's School, separated from its preparatory offspring by several miles of Stour marshes in Kent, had its Senior and

Junior School much closer united once we reached Cornwall. The Senior School took over the Thirties splendour of the clifftop Carlyon Bay Hotel, whilst we Juniors were jammed into the rather more gimcrack structure of the Bayfordbury Hotel opposite. Both hotels had rows of lock-up garages, and these, suitably modified with glass and breeze block, were very useful for changing rooms, classrooms, and even, in the case of the Seniors, a huge chapel in the main servicing building.

The Head of the Junior School was in his element with all the foreseeing of disasters that became necessary. He got us all together and harangued us about some of them. It was likely that we would rush lemming-like over the two hundred foot cliffs, so we were forbidden to go within fifty yards of them. There were caves on the beaches in which we might all become involved in unnatural offences, so they were all put out of bounds. Heinkels were liable to sweep in low from over the sea, machine guns chattering, so that huge dugouts had to be constructed, and when one of the boy wardens blew his whistle, we all had to scamper for them. And, since spies abounded in that rural paradise, we were not to give any military information to anyone, flash torches outside, or refer to the possibility of defeat, which did not, of course, exist. And, if anyone approached us and asked us questions in a heavy German accent, we were to run to the Head as fast as our little legs would carry us.

We had not been in Cornwall more than a couple of terms when, reaching thirteen, I sat an entrance exam to the Senior School. To everyone's surprise, I not only passed this, but was actually awarded some kind of bursary, which reduced the fees payable from Africa by my hard-pressed father to a mere £100 a year. At the time, I think that the Colonial Office was paying him annually only about seven times this.

Most astonished of all at this turn of events was my current Head, who had continued to predict that, when the time came, my new Head Canon Shirley would refuse my candidacy on the grounds of a moral turpitude comparable in scale with that being enjoyed at the time by Eric Gill.

The relief at leaving the Junior School, universally known as the Parrots in the Senior one, was very substantial. I had grown out of the nannyish restrictions and the preoccupation with prolonging childhood as long as possible. The change was enormous. For one thing, the monitors at King's still had the right to beat malefactors as hard and as often as they liked – a privilege which they exploited to the hilt. The masters beat as well, and the most athletic in this respect was the Head, Canon Shirley himself.

Punishment drills were also freely awarded for a range of offences. These usually involved doubling round an improvised barrack square with a rifle above your head, interspersed with press-ups, until you collapsed.

These barbarisms were completely accepted by most of us, and, indeed, their very toughness gave a victim a touch of heroism. And, in return, we were allowed the most amazing freedom. We could bicycle in any direction, go to shops and cinemas, practise unnatural offences in the caves if we wanted to, and generally do anything we fancied outside the hours of formal lessons.

Canon Shirley – known universally as 'Fred' – was, I think, my first encounter with a man enjoying an authentic aura of the supernatural. A qualified barrister who had served as a sub-lieutenant in the Navy before taking Holy Orders at Oxford, he had accepted the arduous job of Head of the King's School on condition that he was made a Canon of Canterbury Cathedral. This role suited his theatrical nature perfectly, and he was never happier than when, dressed in splendid robes, he was thundering out a sermon in the Cathedral. He somehow gave the eerie impression that, like his Maker, he could at the same time read the innermost thoughts of each of the six hundred boys present.

Canon Shirley was glabrously bald, with glittering spectacles over his hypnotic green eyes and the beautifully manicured small hands of a medieval prelate. It was hard to see why his charcoal-grey-pinstriped figure inspired such awe. He had an attention-getting turn of phrase, unquestionably. For example, when we had all assembled in the echoing garage chapel for one of his terrifying sessions of exhortation – known at the time as 'Fred's Fruits' – he began by saying, quite quietly for him, 'Eh, you're all a lot of pustules, sitting in your beds and pulling yourselves about.' From anybody else, such an opening remark would have produced gales of hilarity, but, with Fred, you could have heard a pin drop as we tried to guess where the Fruit was going to lead.

He was an incredible shot with a thrown book. Once I was sitting at the back of a Latin class next to a boy with the not inappropriate name of Slaughter. While Fred, who was a Latin scholar, was writing on the board. Slaughter was telling me a limerick which ended with a reference to human excrement and a pub called the Blue Anchor. As he had a stammer, he made rather heavy weather of laughing and negotiating the last line simultaneously. Like a Western gunfighter, Fred turned from the board, picked up a copy of Hillard and Botting's *Latin Prose Composition* from the desk nearby, and hurled it at Slaughter all in one fluid movement. It caught the unfortunate fifteen-year-old on the bridge of the nose, with enough force to jerk his head backwards and break the window immediately behind. No more limericks were told in that class.

Although my memories of Fred are affectionate, and he showed me some great and unexpected kindnesses, I also had moments of pure terror with him. One such was in a French class held by a strange man called C. E. M. Minns. He had been to Eton and in the Foreign Service, but despite this conformist background, habitually wore electric blue and green suits, and ties that made the rainbow I Zingari ones look monochrome. He had a slight speech defect, and the effect of this was to make it sound as if his whole buccal cavity was full of damp cardboard.

For reasons that I never quite fathomed, I had been consigned to Mr Minns' class, which consisted almost entirely of boys who were dyslexic or mentally subnormal. In desperation, because it was all so dull, I had worked out various techniques which made the hour go a bit quicker. I used to sit next to a boy called Bloomberg, who had also been posted in error into this intellectual graveyard, and he would start the trouble by singing loudly to the tune of 'Onward Christian Soldiers', 'Mr Minns wears flashy suits.'

Minns had no ability at all to maintain discipline, so that he would ignore this rude personal remark, while Bloomberg repeated it louder and louder. Then I would come in on another

61

tack. We all knew that Minns had an inexhaustible taste for the Truth is Stranger than Fiction type of fact, and, indeed, avidly collected scrap books of cuttings of bizarre events.

On this particular day, I had read in a newspaper that some loony had sawn up a bicycle into short lengths and settled down to eat it, tyres and all. I told Minns this, citing chapter and verse from, I think, the *Daily Mirror*. To my great surprise, he did not rise to the bait, merely looking acutely uncomfortable when I repeated the story with embellishments in case he had not heard properly the first time.

We slipped easily into an alternative mode. Minns hated English words pronounced with a French accent, so that you had, for example, to pronounce the word 'mirage' as if it rhymed with 'peerage'. I asked a question involving one of these odious words, and got the usual rebuke, 'When you are speaking English, speak English. When it is French, speak French.' That was good for a minute or two of buffoonery. Then Bloomberg poked me with his elbow, and I let out a loud cry and appealed to Minns to save me from this rough yokel who was assaulting me.

It was all terribly childish, but at the time it seemed better than trying to learn in such company. Anyway I noticed a curious hush behind me. Although our classmates responded to relatively few stimuli, we could generally get a mild titter out of them if we were outrageous enough.

On this occasion, we wriggled about for a good forty minutes, dropped things, hit out at one another and insulted the unfortunate Minns. I noticed that from time to time he seemed to be changing colour, but put this down to the effect of reflections from his brilliant suit on his sallow complexion.

Towards the end of the class, I happened to turn round to direct some shaft at a boy called Crappy Clark who sat behind me. And there, sitting in the back row, pale with anger and spectacles glinting, was Canon Shirley. I was turned to stone as he said in his most terrifying drawl, 'Ah yes, Moreau and Bloomberg, I have been here throughout the class. And you will both come and see me in my study immediately after the end of the lesson.' He vanished, as if back into his genie's bottle. I think that the two of us probably aged twenty years in the twenty minutes before we presented ourselves, exhausted little old men, at the door of his large room on the first floor of the main hotel.

I suppose that if I had ever fallen into the hands of the Gestapo, I might have suffered a more alarming beating, but short of that and actual execution, I cannot remember a session of punishment that was half as grisly. It was made worse by the fact that Fred took Bloomberg first while I looked on, and the wait had destroyed my friend's nerve so completely that he started screaming in a blood-curdling fashion with the first blow and then began running round the room like a decapitated chicken, while the Head stalked him and swiped at the buttock area whenever he saw the opportunity for a snap shot.

Perhaps the fact that I was taken second had one advantage; the remarkably agile Fred had nevertheless used up quite a bit of his daemonic energy and was somewhat out of breath by the time that Bloomberg had collapsed moaning in a corner. Probably to avoid another absurd barnyard chase, he instructed me to lie face downwards on the sofa, so that it was difficult to flee, and he could also rain blows down on me with the minimum of exertion. I have no idea how many times I was hit, but, after a bit, it ceased to hurt, rather as a dentist's drill eventually loses its efficacy in a deep, raw cavity.

10

Aided by the rigorous call-up that was going on, the wartime King's had managed, by the time that I crawled into it via one of the bottom Remove forms, to assemble as its teaching staff one of the most remarkable set of freaks that you could see outside a circus. If we had difficulty keeping ourselves motivated in the Junior School without Mr Burtley, life in the Seniors consisted largely in dodging swishing canes, barbed shafts of sarcasm, blows with the feet, hand and whizzing Latin grammars, as well, occasionally, as expertly groping hands.

One of the Black Belts of the latter activity, albeit briefly, was a man whose short limbs and long neck put me in mind of a two-legged okapi. He came to us with the impeccable record of having been unfrocked as a parson, then subsequently cashiered with ignominy as an officer in the Royal Artillery.

This fellow, whose name was Twiss, took to embarking the more winsome-looking lads in his old Lanchester and driving them out into the numerous remote spots nearby to talk romance. On one occasion late in the evening, he took a lively fellow called Smithers II down to the huge Cornish Riviera Club. This stood half-finished on the beach, and the fine covered tennis and squash courts were used by the school, as was the big swimming pool. It was a balmy night, and Twiss had had in mind a spot of nude bathing, but he got carried away during the undressing procedure. Smithers II took fright, and ran away half-clad across the vast, echoing, dark tennis courts, with Twiss in pursuit shouting 'Smithers II, I love you.'

The chase went on for some time in these Hitchcock-like surroundings, but Smithers finally escaped back to the school on the cliffs above. Shortly afterwards, Twiss was able to add 'dismissed master' to his already dazzling curriculum vitae.

My own Housemaster, a cleric, had a splendid line in repartee, which he possibly got from his claimed ancestor,

Edmund Burke. Once in an English class, after he had made a pronouncement about Shakespeare, he asked me what I thought of his remark. Rather unwisely, and in the current American idiom of the time, I answered, 'You sure slobbered a bibful, Mr Poole.' Without a second's delay, he riposted in his flat Oxford drawl, 'Moreau, I consider you are nearer the age of slobbering bibfuls than I.'

But my favourite recollection of the thankfully non-violent Mr Poole was when a boy called Leary, who has subsequently achieved enormous distinction in the Law, showed a series of his Dali-esque paintings in the school art exhibition. The Art Master, another of our really impressive cranks, whose speech difficulties included loose false teeth, an apparent case of tongue-tie, and no 'r's, stopped in front of the original Leary and began to shake with rage. Leary knew jolly well what the trouble was. The painting was entitled 'A Compresso-pneumonic Telephone', and showed a long, drooping, heavily-veined object straddled across a receiver rest.

'Damn you, Leary,' shouted the Art Master at last, 'that isn't a telephone at all. It's a genital organ.'

'What?' snarled Leary, giving a foretaste of the mock advocate's anger to come, 'as an artist, I am deeply, deeply wounded.'

He snatched the picture from the wall, and ran to see our mutual Housemaster, Mr Poole. Leary caught the latter in one of his moods of Jesuitical cynicism, and, throwing the picture down on the desk in front of him, said furiously, 'Mr Stenhouse has insulted me by calling my telephone a genital organ.' Mr Poole studied the daub for a few moments, then looked up at Leary with an enigmatic smile on his face, saying, 'Well, it doesn't look like my genital organ.'

But the master who affected my life most was a Mr Burnwell. Once, during the blackest part of the war, he erupted into our mathematics classroom, shouting 'There they are, I can see them dying by inches on a raft in mid-Atlantic. You cowardly murderers.'

We congealed at our desks. This was one of his more awesome varieties of class-entry, and it meant that shortly there would be some very nasty incidents and a lot of wailing. Now he glared around, blue eyes smouldering behind their powerful lenses.

'Gentlemen of this great and famous school, I salute you by your standards – British sailors dying for you, and you spit in their faces. Hogs! Hogs!' he barked this out, at the same time doing a little skip of fury and producing from behind his back two slices of mildewed bread – the cause of it all – which he had picked up in the passage.

Another dangerous beginning to the morning was the Burnwell Stealthy Entry. One day I was sitting revolting myself by reading an algebra book, at the same time tapping loudly and auto-hypnotically on the desk with a pen. Suddenly, the harsh voice of Burnwell crooned with mock romanticism right in my ear: 'Ah, drumming the troops to VIC-TOR-Y in the Crimea. Mooreau, VC For Valour, the pride of the Lancers. Beast! Up on your chair, boy. Now another chair upon your head. Mooreau VC, withstanding the torture of the Tartars.'

Now came the worst part. We all knew that Burnwell despised all of us, except, as he frequently told us, three otherwise undistinguished youths named Arnaud, Slimming and Kneller. But it was also well-known among us that he would not actually hit you if your face preserved the unafraid backwoodsman look recommended as the preferred expression by Baden-Powell in his *Scouting for Boys*. Staring ahead of me with an eerie smile on my face, as if I might bellow a Rover Scout's Zulu war chant at any time, I felt my legs beginning to shake with terror. But, after a couple of minutes, during which Burnwell prowled round me waiting for the first un-British snivel, the Headmaster's weekly inspection suddenly marched in, and all the chairs scraped respectfully back. I tried to look as if, in a spasm of awe, I had jumped on my chair, clutching another, and I held my chin to stop a chatter like a haycutter. When the Headmaster departed, Burnwell's train of thought had been interrupted, and he forgot the Crimea, and returned peaceably to quadratic equations.

Sometimes, he sprang in on the balls of his feet, talking conversationally: 'Twenty miles of tubes in you, Waller boy, and you OC-CLUDE fifteen of them by slopping at your desk like that. You'll putrefy, lad.' This was a good sign. He would begin by doing a series of elaborate press-ups in front of us, ending by rising from floor level on one leg, explaining that his extraordinary physical condition at sixty came from his mother, who, buried in the ruins of her house in Liverpool at the age of eighty-eight, had stayed alive for two days by eating a box of candles.

Burnwell was a tall, long-legged man with a scholarly stoop, and an immense white head full of calculated crankiness. His terrifying unpredictability made him the best disciplinarian that I have ever met, and I have no doubt that he could keep order in a class of female baboons if necessary.

Using the same methods, he also taught chemistry and biology in a vast, creaking wooden hut that had been erected for the purpose when the school was evacuated. In the floor of the biology half, he had constructed a trap through which the remains of dissected dogfish and other sacrifices could be hurled when finished with. On the dry earth underneath, a formidable heap built up, brilliantly luminous at night, and producing a stench like that in the Tanzanian villages where the same vintage crocodile would be dug up for a feast every year.

Apart from seemingly having no sense of smell, Burnwell actually liked poison gas. Unnecessarily often, he made chlorine, ritualistically filling the laboratories' largest flask with hydrochloric acid and manganese dioxide. As the heavy green cloud rolled towards us, Burnwell began to lecture, twitching with pleasure.

'Observe the slow advance of the gas, and its affinity for the floor. A beautiful colour, is it not?' And he would rasp on until only his glasses could be seen glinting through the moss-coloured fog, and we were all quietly choking into our handkerchiefs. The important thing here was not to move from your seat until the official evacuation order was given. A boy called Sharp once ran in panic for the door. Burnwell caught him in six strides, snarling, 'Ha, yellow, are you?' And Sharp then had to stand for minutes over the belching flask, while ex-Captain Burnwell explained slowly how in the Great War his men had preferred *As-phyx-iation* to dishonour by fleeing.

When the Government appealed for Gas Officers, Burnwell was one of the first volunteers. He splashed yellow detector paint everywhere, had sessions of making every known gas so that we would know what they smelt like, and made the gasmask testing van call almost weekly.

On these occasions, the whole school, bemasked, had to file slowly through the horrid gaschamber. Once I met Burnwell inside. I regarded him timorously through the condensation on my plastic eyeholes. Then he lifted his gasmask off and trumpeted, 'And now we will take off our masks and see what we are missing.' He inhaled the tear gas deeply and noisily, fixing me with a steely gaze. I took off mine, and, with heaving chest, made a pretence of breathing, while tears spurted from my eyes. Presently, however, anoxia made me breathe the gas, and I began retching and choking. But I remembered that my chemistry book said that, if I could survive the first few minutes, I would almost cease to notice the effects – whereas I had to meet Burnwell every day at mathematics. I turned my sightless eye in the direction of Burnwell's heavy breathing, and, between agonizing bouts of coughing, said 'It's lovely, isn't it, sir?'

Suddenly, I felt his sinewy hand on my head, and he said almost kindly, 'Why, you're not yellow, boy. You may go now.'

After that, for a short time, I joined the mysterious Burnwell élite. Even on 'Cowardly Hog' mornings, Burnwell's collective accusations of cowardice or bestiality would end '. . . except for Arnaud, Slimming, Kneller and Mooreau.' Hitherto statistically the most frequent victim on Stealthy Entry mornings, I now watched from the luxury of my private Valhalla my classmates being immunised to the harsh unfairness of life.

But this honeymoon could not continue, and a few months later came the moment when he changed my life. After School Certificate – the early equivalent of O-Levels – it was seemingly recognized that I was not quite so moronic as they had thought, and I was promoted seven forms in one go into the Lower Sixth. By now, I had decided to do medicine, and went confidently into the first chemistry class which was to be one of my three subjects for A-Levels, or Higher Certificate as they were called then.

Somehow during that morning, while Burnwell was out of the lab, I got into a fight using the washbottles off the benches.

Directing a long, hissing jet at my neighbour, I never heard Burnwell creeping up behind me until suddenly he seized me by the hair and dragged me to the floor.

As I lay there unable to move without considerable danger of instant alopecia, he addressed the rest of the class in a leisurely fashion about the innervation of the scalp, capillary reflexes, pityrosporum ovale, dandruff, and, indeed, most matters relevant to the head that was suffering under his iron fingers. When I finally got dazedly to my feet, I left the lab never to return, hurried to the Headmaster and told him that I had changed my mind and now I wanted to do languages and the Law at University instead. 'Eh, you little pustule,' he said cheerily, digging me affectionately in the solar plexus with his extended fingers, 'you'll miss Mr Burnwell's funny little ways, y'know.'

11

One of our nicest, kindest masters was J. B. Harris, who had an unusual, bow-legged walk. This was always said to be because he had left his goolies on the barbed wire while winning the MC in the first Great War. Whether this was true or not, he had preserved an unshakeably sweet temper. Another very well-intentioned man was Captain Egerton-Jones, also a bemedalled survivor of the same conflict. For some reason, the layout of his teeth and tongue caused him to whistle quite loudly on the sibilants, so that he was universally known an Eggy-Whistle. And, although one of our favourite sports was to ask questions about such subjects as the defenestration of Prague to get a shrill sound from him, he never seemed to be provoked.

Much more diabolical was Mr Bolingbroke, who really dreamed of playing Hamlet to huge audiences in the West End, and who in fact ultimately became a professional actor – perhaps when parental complaints drove him out of teaching. Of all the aggressive masters, Bolingbroke was the king. When roused, his face would go scarlet under its iron grey curls, and veins would palpitate on his temples. As a bookthrower, he ranked just below the Headmaster. But some of his athletic feats of persecution could only have been performed by an actor or a gymnast.

Once a friend of mine called Matthew, sitting next to me, became so unnerved while translating out loud from the *Aeneid* that he began to stammer and stutter. With one bound, the incensed Bolingbroke leapt up on the wretched boy's desk and swore that, for every mistake, he would kick Matthew in the face. This he proceeded to do with the toe of his finely embossed brogue.

Like Burnwell, he was also an expert hairpuller, and had been known to drag a boy to the front of the class by this means, and then bang his head against the blackboard. There was a distinct tendency in the school to plead with the authorities for transfer out of Bolingbroke's alarmingly violent classes.

A saturnine man called Olssen, whose white hair grew in a sort of tonsure, making it impossible to guess his age, could also be rather dangerous in class. A bit like Burnwell, he was also the master of the surprise attack. A boy would clown behind Olssen's back, and then settle down, believing that he had passed unremarked. But he rarely had. Olssen would work his way round the room, talking reassuringly like a vet approaching a restive horse, until he was abeam the unsuspecting clown. Then, abruptly, he would deliver a stinging blow to the face.

One of the Housemasters, Piggy Reynolds, frequently claimed to classes that his invulnerability in peace and in war came from wearing a leather jockstrap. Frankly, we never had the opportunity of checking that this was the source of his staying power, but he could be an ugly customer on a bad day.

For a number of reasons, the school Chaplain was in a class by himself. Estimates of his gross weight varied between twenty-four and thirty stone, although he was only of average height. He accentuated his formidable volume by always wearing a black cassock with a thick belt like a horse's girth round his maximum circumference. Archbishop Temple, who had a smaller version of the same figure, once said that his voluminous surplices used to come back from the laundry listed as 'One Bell-Tent'. Our Chaplain's must have done the same. His face was beefy and red, surmounted by short, curly dark hair, with a synod of chins running for cover into the neckline of his cassock. He was invariably known to masters and boys as 'The Tank'.

Perhaps the Tank's most remarkable characteristic was his unselfconsciouness. He walked his gigantic stomach about the school as if he was sitting in the prow of a ship, and all the titters and comments passed him completely by. Like many very fat men, he moved quietly and quite easily on his thick soled shoes, propelled by calf muscles like those of an Olympic weightlifter on steroids.

He claimed to be a first cousin of the beautiful, stylish and Heseltine-haired Rupert Brooke, and sometimes would gasp out a few lines of Grantchester or the Chilterns to accentuate the likeness. His voice was a rasping squeak, as if it was being forced out of him under great pressure, and sounding not at all as one would expect from a romantic poet buried in some corner of a foreign field.

When I was about fifteen, a friend told me that he had tasted Communion wine, and it was so delicious that he had had himself confirmed, and got up an hour early every Sunday in order to enjoy a gulp or two from the chalice. In fact, he thought it was even nicer than his previous favourite food, which was mayonnaise sucked off a knitting needle dipped directly into the bottle. So I decided to join these mini-carousals on Sundays, and told the Tank that I wanted to be confirmed.

Being unmarried and without any apparent romantic affiliation, he spent a lot of time being helpful in his room, which was on the first landing of the hotel, and enabled him to get a panoramic view of pretty well everything that was going on. One of the little services that he was glad to perform was the loan of a cobbler's last to anyone whose shoes needed repair – footgear was rationed, and we were all obliged to walk miles every day, so that frequent DIY repairs were necessary.

Anyway, on the day of my first confirmation class, I was busy praying into the seat of a big armchair ('nibbing' was the rather odd school slang for this activity) when, abruptly, there was a terrible crash in the grate and the whole room filled with soot. Some ungrateful boy had borrowed the Tank's last just before the class, and had returned it by the somewhat unusual route of climbing on to the roof of the hotel and dropping it down the chimney. The Tank was not amused.

I am sorry to say that, at about this time, the Facts of Life reared their head again. I had assumed when I first came into the school that everyone must have been told that I was in possession of this dreadful information, but this proved not to be the case. In fact, a number of efforts were made to help me to understand the whole thing. It started in one of Burnwell's biology classes.

On that particular day his tall, spare figure gave no sign of the agitation that sometimes gripped it. 'To-day,' he intoned quite cheerily, gripping the blackboard pointer that served him as assegai, goad, club and cane, 'we will be studying the mysterious fact that the genetic hereditaments of humankind are carried about in tiny crumpled bags by hundreds of millions of despicable oafs like you, who are so unappreciative that they actually use them as terms of abuse. What have I just said, Slimming?'

'That we're unappreciative oafs who abuse the things that we've got, sir.'

'And what are those things?' asked Burnwell unpleasantly.

'Dunno, I'm afraid, sir,' answered Slimming, bracing himself for an assault which, to his surprise, did not come.

'Mooreau, what am I talking about, then?'

'I think you were referring to the epididymis,' I said rather prissily. Only the absence of horn-rimmed spectacles prevented me from looking like Form 5D's swot when talking about my favourite subject.

'Oh you do, do you?' said Burnwell, his early warning system of a twitching mouth becoming activated, 'well, I wasn't, you little show-off.'

'The cells of Leydig, then?' I said, taking a deep breath of dogfish-laden air, and thinking of all the past parental trouble that had been taken to equip me for this moment.

'How could a bloody cell be a little crumpled bag?' he snarled, 'and when did you ever hear a revolting little boy like you shouting "Leydig cells" when someone was talking rubbish? Are you trying to be funny, boy?'

'No sir, not at all sir,' I said pleadingly, noting a few more danger signs, like Burwell's top denture descending with a clack on the plosive consonants, 'I thought all cells were bags of a sort.'

'Well, I will teach you the difference, boy. Come and stand here.' He indicated a spot just in front of his podium. I moved to it, and stood swaying a little as Burnwell rummaged behind his bench, emerging with a brown paper bag on which the words MAZAWATTEE TEA were emblazoned. He proffered it to me, saying, 'That is a bag, boy. To help you remember, put it on your head and stand still.'

I pulled it down to my eyes. It had obviously held fishy corpses at some time.

'Right down over your nose,' he said wheedlingly. Reluctantly I blindfolded myself. If you have never stood unsighted, with a stunningly fishy container on your head, while a violent eccentric prowls round you with a weapon, you can't imagine how difficult it is. It was quite a relief when he poked me twice on the navel with the pointer, then led me back to my desk where I sat half-asphyxiated while the lesson on reproduction went on.

Strangely enough, one of the most onerous tasks undertaken by the Tank was also the passing on of the Facts of Life. Since the whole idea of his actually performing, or even catching sight of his own external sexual panoply, was quite risible, we all thought that his grasp of the subject must have been wholly academic.

One day, about this time, as I became manifestly pubescent, I saw the Tank heave into view down the cinder path to the classrooms. As he eyed me, he noticed the raw stigmata of primitive shaving on my cheeks. Stopping, he said, 'Moreau, it's clearly time that we had a talk. Meet me in my bathroom at 7 p.m. on Thursday this week.'

I knew from the others that this curious tryst was not necessarily sinister. The Tank simply found it more agreeable when explaining the reproductive system to have you seated in front of him, wearing only a pair of games shorts and in his warm bath.

I duly turned up on the Thursday, sporty shorts safely in place, and ran a bath of the right temperature for a long stay. He sank down on a stool, so that it disappeared completely under his cassock. He began his talk, versions of which were favourites for imitation among initiates.

'What I am going to say may puzzle you, even shock you. That is why you are in a relaxing bath. It will also remind you that life started in the sea. God, in his prodigality, first instituted congress between males and females with the two elements floating towards one another without bodily contact. But, when life emerged from the ocean, he had to think of another solution.' He stopped, grimacing a little as he thought of the works of the Almighty, before adding, 'Any questions so far?'

Resisting the temptation to express shock and horror about

his tale to date, I merely said, 'No, thank you, please go on, sir.'

'Well,' he squeaked, 'with the flowers, the bee acts as the Heavenly messenger between the two loving entities. With human beings, you carry the sacred equivalent of the bee inside your games trousers.' He groaned slightly at the thought. I realised that I was beginning to giggle helplessly, concentric circles of agitated bathwater spreading out from my fluttering diaphragm.

'Any questions?' he asked again.

'Yes,' I said, suddenly getting a grip of myself and fed up with the terrible complexes that adults seemed to have about these rather attractive matters which I had learned at my mother's knee when our pet monkey was born, 'would it be true to say that the genetic hereditaments of the world are carried about in a tiny crumpled bag, number one. And, secondly, would you say that it's the same for Colobus monkeys?'

The Tank's reaction did not disappoint me. 'That's blasphemy, boy,' he snarled, suddenly quite ungodly as he leaned forward to slap my face.

12

I would not like you to think that this unrelenting war with authority prevented us from having a tremendous amount of fun. Many of us had quite fanatical hobbies, which included aircraft recognition, birdwatching, writing poetry, keeping kestrels and buzzards to hawk with, eating food stolen from the kitchens, making things from shoes to sailing boats, learning *Bradshaw's Railway Guide* page by page, self abuse and transvestism, as well as playing a huge variety of games, some official and some not.

One of my favourite pastimes was brickfighting. For this, about ten of us used to retire to the abundant local woods, and five of the group would set up a defended position. The other five would attack it. Of the attackers, some would hurl large stones from a distance on a mortar trajectory, so that they descended vertically from the blue heaven into the ring of defenders. And others would advance sending their smaller stones hurtling in the flatter arc favoured nowadays by hooligans throughout the world.

All of us were struck, some frequently, and it always puzzled me why no one was ever mortally injured. I suppose we were a rather battle-seasoned group who indulged in this lethally infantile pastime, and we had got used over the months to watching our front and the sky simultaneously for fast-moving missiles.

I had another hobby which grew on me steadily over my teens. Right through to the time that I became a purple-gowned monitor, with the power to thrash the insolent, I held my trousers up with a Girl Guides' belt purloined from my sister. The reason that it suited me so well was that its length was garnished with hooks and rings on which accoutrements and weapons could conveniently be hung. And I made more than full use of them, so that, if I didn't hug myself tightly as I walked into Chapel, I clanked like a medieval man-at-arms.

The contents of the belt's little purse were particularly historic. Before the war, I had been shown round the attics of a great house in Wellington, Somerset, by the ageing beldam who owned it. An ancient percussion gun caught my attention. Around it were stacked boxes of verdigrissed copper caps for the breech mechanism. As an acquisitive schoolboy, I was thrilled to be given a box of a hundred, and for years afterwards carried a purseful of these lovely little explosive items just in case I needed to arm a breechloader in a hurry.

Crammed into the same purse, I also carried a flat tin that had once held sticking plaster. Now it was half-filled with a yellowish powder that I had cautiously mixed with a feather in the chemistry lab. With its potassium chlorate base, it was highly explosive, and I cannot now quite understand why it missed its opportunity over all those months of blowing off my right leg.

At that time, the German *Wehrmacht* was locked in combat with the gallant French Resistance just across the Channel, and we all knew that any night the rustling of wavelets on the beach could suddenly turn to the scrunch of the bows of assault craft. I felt that we had to practise for the possibility that shortly we might all be going underground, so I used to lead intrepid parties of would-be patriots through the woods to the Par to St Austell railway line. There, we would put a few grains from my precious plaster tin on the bright metal track. The satisfyingly loud reports from under the great driving wheels of the next steam engine told us that, when the time came, we would be able to match the train-wrecking efforts of our French cousins.

A friend of mine and I had decided that it would also be a desirable thing if we could set fire to the landing craft full of steel-helmeted SS men as they nosed in to the shingle below our school. So, after consulting the section on incendiary devices in a chemical encyclopaedia, he stole some metallic sodium from the lab, where it was stored immersed in inert oil.

In his school locker, deprived of its protection, it fumed and hissed all the time while we waited day and night for the invasion armada. Eventually, we decided that we would have to get rid of it in a properly organized military exercise.

Having pushed a large piece of driftwood out to sea to represent the enemy, we climbed to the top of the cliff. Then I hurled down an open bottle of lighter fuel, while he sent his highly reactive chemical weapon whizzing down a couple of hundred feet. It struck the water well clear of both the plank and the petrol, rushed about in furious circles roaring and steaming, then blew up with a satisfying boom and a column of orange flame. Though our aim was poor, we decided exultantly that even if the invaders were members of the *Leibstandart Adolf Hitler*, they would have second thoughts about invading a shore that was clearly so vigorously defended.

This experience made me consider carrying some sodium about with me as well. But, with my new insight into what might happen if, say, I was struck in the pocket by a water bomb, I reluctantly decided that it was our patriotic duty to leave the sodium safely in its oil until we heard the warning whistles of the Home Guard presaging a landing, then we would instantly burgle the chemistry lab by climbing through Burnwell's trapdoor and the stinking dogfish. We reckoned that this act of heroism should be good for a mention in dispatches.

Anyway, I was distracted by being given a handful of yellow phosphorus, and for one day sat proudly in class, with the white fumes of phosphorus pentoxide pouring out of the pocket of my black suit. I was excited by the thought that, put carefully into closed bottles of petrol, it would make perfect Molotov cocktails for us to defend ourselves with.

Next day, however, a spoilsport called Binbrook came up to me with a copy of an early medical textbook from the library, and showed me a repulsive engraving of a man who seemed to have had such a surprise that his jaw had done more than simply drop open; it had dropped off.

'Do you know what this is?' he asked unpleasantly.

'Well, it says underneath that it's a case of Fossy Jaw,' I answered.

'That's right,' he said, 'it was very common among matchmakers in the early nineteenth century. In our form, we aren't Victorian workmen making lucifers. We don't particularly mind if your jaw rots off, but we think that we would prefer to keep ours intact for the time being. So, get rid of your bloody phosphorus before we do both you and it a mischief.'

Regretfully, and feeling that I was letting the country down, I gave the attractively opalescent stuff back to its previous owner.

Then I had a brief flirtation with another explosive – nitrogen tri-iodide – which I could make in quite large quantities during break in the lab. It proved to blow up so easily, however, that it would sometimes even do so untouched and while drying out after manufacture.

Put on the floor, gently crepitating as it matured, it would give warning of the approach of anybody with a series of angry little explosions, staining the marauder's feet or shoe-soles at the same time with brown iodine. But, no matter how carefully I walked with the purple crystals in my pocket, they always blew up, and the sewing room became quite puzzled by my frequent attendance for the repair of tattered brown holes in the lining of my black suit.

Sadly, I realized that the potential military use of this explosive was probably in the same category as that Wellingtonian troop that frightened the great General more than they did the enemy.

About this time, there occurred an incident which cured me, at least temporarily, of my love of bombs. In *War Illustrated*, I had read details of how Sepp Dietrich, Hitler's former chauffeur and the head of his bodyguard, selected the necessary perfect specimens for that force and his Führer. Not only did they have to be six feet and a half inch tall; they also had to prove that they had no stoppings in their perfect Teutonic teeth. Then they had to go and stand in a clearing in the woods, put a coal scuttle *Wehrmacht* helmet on their blond heads, take the pin out of a hand grenade, and balance it on top of the metal. They stood perfectly still while the five second fuse burned, and then it went off with a terrifying bang. The instructor supervising this act of foolhardy courage would hide himself behind a substantial tree, while counting loudly. A stretcher party hid behind another tree.

If the would-be recruit did not shake too much, and stood the bomb properly on its end cap, he apparently survived this rigorous procedure with no more than concussion and a lasting deafness, which, for some reason the *Wehrmacht* medics seemed to accept. If the thing fell off at the wrong moment, then that was the end of the aspirations of the young hopeful.

Anyway this seemed to me to be an incomparable means of celebrating the passage of puberty. I couldn't get hold of a Mills bomb, and, in any case, I had doubts whether a good British grenade would go off as harmlessly as its Kraut equivalent. So I made up my own fiendish device. I have to admit that my hands trembled a little as I tamped explosive into the centre of an old lavatory roll.

'Go on, that's nothing like the size of the gun cotton charge in a Mills bomb,' said one of my friends, watching me spoon in black powder from stolen shotgun cartridges, and anxious for a human sacrifice.

It was clearly a spectator sport and, since a crowd standing on the beach and waiting for me to disintegrate might attract the attention of the coastguards, we went as usual into the woods.

I was wearing a battered Tommy's helmet from the Great War, *Berlin Here We Come* still painted round the crown. It feels terribly lonely, standing in a clearing with a high explosive contrivance upright on your occiput. I had made a nuncupatory will leaving everything to my sister, just in case I was vaporized. I felt sure that for testamentary purposes this was Active Service. Then I took out a box of Swan Vestas, lit a roaring length of fuse lost from a local tin mine, and balanced the lavatory roll on the umbilical rivet on top of the battle bowler.

Muffled shouts of encouragement came from behind the trees all round me. Someone even tried to make me laugh as the orange fuse hissed out its choking fumes.

'Bloody Hell, I'm going,' shouted some faintheart, and crashed away through the rhododendron bushes. I couldn't answer anything, for fear that just opening my mouth would make the fat cracker fall and blow my feet off. The wait was awful. It was almost a relief when there was a kick like a stallion to my crown, a violet flash all round me, and an ear-destroying bang. The bomb had blown out its wooden base plug, and soared as a rocket into the branches of a fir tree, where it caused a small fire. I was too dazed even to feel triumphant as my relieved audience crowded round me as one might a Rugby field injury. I just sank to the pine needles, head aching. Now I understood why the German elite went into battle afraid of nothing except their own training methods.

Thinking about this afterwards, I concluded that bombs were somehow untidy. Handguns were really the thing. One day, I was taking a Sten gun to pieces in the school armoury, goaded by the visiting sergeant who had taught us bayonet drill while shouting, 'Kill, kill,' through the grim portcullis of his Xylonite teeth. It was obvious that the whole crude mechanism could be imitated using only a hacksaw, hand-drill and file. At the same time, it could be miniaturized so as to fire .22 cartridges lost from the school shooting range.

I went to work, my study desk becoming a munitions factory on which lay more swarf than Latin Proses. The first firing was an emotional affair in the school vegetable room, which was below ground, and therefore reasonably safe from spoilsports. A knot of teenage disbelievers collected well behind the new weapon, which was tied to the handle of a garden fork jammed into a pile of beetroots.

The first few jerks of my firing cord were resisted by the stiff new trigger mechanism, and were greeted with derisive moans from the onlookers. So I gave a despairing tug. The fork reeled backwards, and the gun banged like a squeaky twelve-bore. As the watchers behind collapsed to the floor with histrionic alarm, a bullet buried itself in the ceiling.

Rather to my surprise, the barrel hadn't blown apart, and indeed, the whole thing, now blued with gunsmoke, looked quite intact and purposeful. I realized that I was now properly armed to receive the alien barbarians that Churchill talked about.

Next time I fired the gun, I held it nonchalantly in my right hand, which may account for the fact that nowadays I hear slightly less well through my right ear than my left one. The new weapon, minus its detachable butt, was about the size of the Jumbo Fountain Pen with which it was fashionable to distend your breast pocket in those days, so that I was able to carry it about all the time.

One day, as I was sitting in a particularly boring class about Wordsworth and the pantheists, an idea suddenly burgeoned.

81

My little pocket howitzer would be perfect for murdering German officers at close range as they sipped *Sekt* in French bars, or stood kissing their collaborating girl friends 'Goodnight', to the strains of *Lili Marlene*.

So I tore a sheet out of my exercise book, and wrote in my best hand boldly at the top: MOST SECRET AND FOR YOUR EYES ONLY. To the General Commanding the War Office, from Lance-Corporal David Moreau, S45, OTC King's School, Canterbury, but currently in the Carlyon Bay Hotel, Cornwall.

'Sir,
    It has come to my attention that there is a requirement for a covert weapon, to be used by patriots for assassinating members of the German Armed Forces, both in Occupied countries, and in England, should they avoid the pitchforks of the Home Guard. Strictly between ourselves, I have invented a highly effective miniature gun for this purpose, which I shall be glad to demonstrate to you in the greatest secrecy if you would be prepared to come down to Cornwall, or send a Staff car to bring me up to London. A brief technical specification is enclosed. Neither my Headmaster nor any of his subordinates know of this, and I would be beaten to a pulp if they knew of my War Work.
                I look forward to your news by return,
                        Yours faithfully,
                    Lance Corporal Moreau'

As the weeks passed, I began to worry about the lack of response. Perhaps with typically vile adult solidarity, the General had ratted to the school's management. Perhaps the Special Branch had already been instructed to root out this homicidal schoolboy, and have him put away in a Borstal somewhere. Eventually, after giving up all hope of being recognized as one of the Architects of Final Victory, I got a letter from a Major at the War House.

'Dear Corporal Moreau' (he had written, unwittingly promoting me a grade) 'We have read your letter with interest and surprise, and it has been shown to experts close to the Prime Minister' – I chortled as I read that – 'We are impressed by your enthusiasm and fighting spirit' – 'Kill, kill,' I shouted to the empty room, baring my teeth like the sergeant major. The letter went on: 'However, most of us feel that the time is past when significant numbers of Germans will have to be murdered in English pubs, although we will certainly bear it in mind for French estaminets and similar establishments. You must be aware that escape would be difficult when using a weapon which fires only one shot. Thank you again. Say not the struggle naught availeth. Keep it up. Jolly good show.

I am, Corporal, Yours truly,

H. Brown, Major'

'What an unimaginative desk-basher,' I thought. If only he knew that orders from my fellow schoolboys alone for this wonderful means of personal protection would keep me busy filing and drilling for the rest of the year.

13

When I look back, I am never quite sure whether I learnt anything at all useful in the official classes at school. Patchily in the English lessons, I understood what oxymorons and palindromes were, but I have never consciously used them, and only occasionally feel superior when I hear the endless parades of celebrity-nonentities asked to define them in quiz programmes, Algebra remained incomprehensible, and, although in those days I could solve quadratic equations quicker than most, this was only because I had craftily memorised a formula which did this, and I never saw the utility, or found any situation in which they could be used.

With my painfully acquired Latin, I have deciphered a few tombstones, and grasped Latin tags a little quicker than some when studying law, but I doubt whether the tortuous man-hours spent in learning defective and deponent verbs were well-applied. More useful has been learning Hamlet by heart – at Cambridge I came to play several of the minor parts, and could do them with only a quick brushing up. Grinding through Matthew Arnold gave me a nice little reservoir of apposite quotations, including what I believe to be the ugliest couplet in the English language:

Who prop, thou ask'st, in these bad days, my mind,
He much, the old man who, clearest soul'd of men . . .

In geography, we spent hours learning the boundaries of the counties, and what river each county town was on. Much of this knowledge became redundant when Ted Heath decided to destabilise the shires and the British people by abolishing ancient ones like Rutland and Monmouth, and even attempt to move my own house into Berkshire – I am still prepared to put up with a day's delay in my post for the pleasure of putting the historic Buckinghamshire name in my address.

The Tank gave scripture classes which were frankly absurd. With his tongue protruding with the effort, he would write the whole lesson in tiny handwriting from top to bottom of the blackboard, and we would then copy it out. Having his back turned for ten minutes at a time was an invitation to all kinds of silent misbehaviour, from throwing darts to attempting to undo the flies of the boy next door, and the mindless copying of all the trite verbiage meant that most of us never remembered a word of what he had said. But we all enjoyed his rambling explanation of how there could be Three Persons and one God, so that he would often be asked to go over this bit of dogma again.

In history, the slim lampoon *1066 and All That* taught me almost all that I knew. This may have been partly the consequence of the time that we devoted to encouraging Captain Eggy-Whistle to produce his fluting sound, rather than working. Also, the history book that was standard in the school made the mistake of adding colourful bits of knowledge in footnotes on every page. Having inherited a certain dreaminess from my mother, together with a love of the bizarre, I found that, when a footnote told me that the Duke of Suffolk was taken off a cross-Channel packet and had his head cut off in a small boat with half a dozen strokes of a rusty sword, only these grisly details stuck in my mind, to the exclusion of who he was, or why he was crossing to France.

Perhaps the exception was languages. A little man called 'Peeny' Voigt did a rarely good job in teaching French by what is now known as the 'direct' method, in other words, he conducted the class in the language itself which, as one might have expected, was more successful than grimly mining through its syntax and vocabulary, as was done with Latin.

I didn't really get a fair run at the sciences, because I was trapped for so long in the bottom class with Crappy Clark, Bloggy Apps and a fellow known simply as Enderbum, and it was all we could to to get past the simplest experiments and lighting our Bunsen burners. And I stormed out of Burnwell's more senior class for ever before he really taught me anything relevant – even if I could ever have got the information into my head past the fear barrier.

Music had also largely passed me by. I had taught myself to play the old piano in one of the classrooms, until one day when I was loudly negotiating a rough bit of jazz, and Piggy Reynolds suddenly materialized, trembling with the energetic rage that no doubt came from wearing a leather jockstrap. He forbad me ever to touch another school piano. I was also in the school choir for a short while, until being fired by Mr Phillips, the choirmaster, for becoming hysterical when the boy soprano standing next to me farted as he hit a top note.

I did however learn a tremendous amount about explosives, and another subject which intrigued me: the relatively large number of compounds that are naturally luminous. Certainly, too, I learned a lot about human courage and cowardice – when you watch a few people being really thrashed, and go through the same treatment yourself, you soon appreciate that the bravest human beings are not necessarily the most macho ones.

I learned a lot from the brickfights, too, and from the more sophisticated form of warfare that succeeded them. Most of us had acquired air pistols and rifles by now, and a remote corner of the hotel garden, which we called Delville Wood after the bloody First World War battle, was the scene of many grim encounters when we used them on one another over the months. One or two of my cronies were VC material; they would charge several accurately firing air rifles at speed, collecting slugs in the legs and body on the way, and press on into a hand-to-hand encounter. Although I regularly got shot myself, at least twice in the face, I wasn't brave enough for the fearless dash over open ground under fire, and I admired those who were.

It was interesting to see how quickly boys become men once puberty is passed. Burnwell was the master in charge of swimming, and on one occasion a boy called Henry Hannah got severe cramp while attempting to swim a Silver Medal exam. He had to be pulled in agony out of the water, quite incapable of managing another stroke. Characteristically, Burnwell came and leaned over the recumbent form by the poolside to say, 'You didn't have cramp at all, boy. You're yellow, that's all.'

Hannah was of volatile Irish extraction, and now he gasped through clenched teeth, 'Wait till I can walk again, then come round behind the changing sheds with me and we'll see who is yellow.' Burnwell laughed at him, but readily agreed. Shortly,

Hannah pulled himself painfully to his feet, and the two of them disappeared from our view, Hannah the shorter by nearly six inches. A couple of minutes later they reappeared, Burnwell with a splendid black eye, limping, and holding his shattered glasses in his hand.

The same sudden horn-locking aggression became apparent in other ways. One of them was the Light Fusing War. Two of the senior boys were the school's electricians, and very good at the job. Then, at the beginning of one term, as the Headmaster came into Chapel for morning prayers, and the main lights were switched on, they all fused with a loud bang, and morning prayers had to be conducted in the gloom that resulted. It appeared that a little disc of metal, put under a bulb in one of the sockets, had produced this exciting result.

This was the first of many such incidents, until a few major events occurred without sudden darkness supervening, and we all became accustomed to groaning loudly several times during prep in the evening when abrupt blackness made work impossible, and encouraged us to attack our neighbours to while away the time until repairs were effected. It was rumoured that the light-fuser was a senior boy who was revenging himself for not being promoted to school monitor, but no culprit was ever discovered, and after months of disorder, the campaign stopped as suddenly as it had begun.

A similar event was the stealing of the School Steward's car. He was a greasy individual, who nevertheless succeeded in acquiring quite a lot of sweets, food and general supplies that were in short supply at the time. He owned a smart Standard saloon, which was parked out in front of the school. One evening it disappeared, and was gone until the early hours of the morning. When it was returned, the tyres and brakes had had weeks of wear, and the petrol gauge needle was on zero. There were several reports from the police and others of it being seen racing through remote villages a long way from the school. But the demon driver was never caught.

The school made well-meaning attempts to broaden our educational background by inviting down preachers, lecturers and musicians of very varying quality.

I remember the Vicar of Liskeard, as soon as he had got our

attention, suddenly whipping out from under his cassock the large sword that he had carried in a previous existence as a cavalryman. Then, predictably, he preached a sermon about beating swords into ploughshares.

Another cleric, also thinking to impress a schoolboy congregation, imitated chuffing trains, complete with guard's whistle, in order to illustrate a sermon on the text: 'My treadings had well-nigh slipt.' The reference was to a time that he had tried to board a moving carriage, and a porter had caught him as he was about to fall under the wheels. Needless to say, he saw the hand of God in this event.

But the best of the sermons was given by Baldock the school gardener, an old retainer and non-conformist lay preacher from a Kentish village. His text, delivered with dialect 'r's, was: 'One. The world is upside down. Two. It's got to be put rightside up again. Three. We're the chaps to do the job.' This was subsequently immortalized in every impromptu schoolboy sermon.

Some of the musicians were of great quality – Joan and Valery Trimble, Gerald Moore of *Am I too Loud?* fame, and Leon Goossens, for example – and we wondered how on earth they had been attracted down to the wilds of Cornwall.

Shortly after the invasion, General Montgomery (as he was then) came down to talk to us. He was, of course, an old boy of the school, and, indeed, one of its Governors. We listened enthralled to both a statement of his overall military philosophy – 'Never make a move to attack the enemy until you have built up overwhelming superiority, no matter how restive the politicians get' – and a vivid recounting of details of his campaigns.

One of these was the story of how he had the main road into Holland reconnoitred at a time when there was a theory that the Germans had retreated, and the weather was too bad for aerial reconnaissance. A brave Humber armoured car crew volunteered to race up the road for a dozen miles and have a look-see. By the time that the seven-ton vehicle passed through the British front line, it was already doing over seventy miles an hour. They tore on, gaining further speed, for the agreed distance through empty countryside, then turned peacefully, to come back and report that they had not even been fired on, and the country seemed to be deserted.

While Montgomery was talking, a large Army lorry drove up outside the thin asbestos walls of the lecture-theatre chapel, and stopped there, big diesel clanking. Monty tolerated it for perhaps a minute, trying to make his thin voice heard above the racket, then snapped testily to a boy in the front row, 'Go out and tell that lorry driver to either go away, or to stop his engine.' We heard the boy duly shout his message above the roar of the engine, beginning, 'General Montgomery says . . .'

At that time, the General had become legendary throughout the Army, and his name was often taken in vain, so that we were not surprised to hear the military driver bawl back, 'Go'n tell the bloody General, son, that Private Smiffs' too busy winnin' the effing war ter stop.'

Decisive as ever, Monty marched to the door and appeared outside, eight rows of medals and the two badges on his Tank Corps beret gleaming. The terrified soldier took one look, then roared for the horizon.

I did a lot of acting, too, which stood me in good stead in after life. Because I was fair-complexioned, the first roles that I had tended to be female. In fact, I really disliked tittuping round the stage in high heels, with socks stuffed into a bra borrowed from the matron, but it gave me an edge that not every one had, so I put up with it. I am probably one of the few people who has played both Mrs Eynsford Hill and her son Freddie in successive productions of *Pygmalion*.

One night, we played *The Last of Mrs Cheyney* in the Methodist Hall in the tiny local fishing village of Charlestown. The play includes a few mild oaths – damns and bloodys mostly – but they proved too ungodly for the staunch nonconformists of the place, and after the first few curses had been followed by gasps and muttering, the Harbourmaster, who had a mane of white hair like John the Baptist, stood up in the audience and bawled, 'Hey, cut out them adjectives, if you don't mind.' There was an astonished silence on the stage for a few seconds, then we pressed on, each of us rapidly revising in our minds the rest of our parts.

One of the problems of the female impersonator was that, in a resolutely all-male society like King's in those days, you tended to have older chaps trying to date you for a few days after each play, as I understand they did in prisoner-of-war camps. Our exposure to girls was absolutely minimal – apart from the cleaning ladies and the Headmaster's acidulous middle-aged secretary, the only specimen I remember on the premises was an unfortunate under-secretary nicknamed 'Bweastless Bwenda' by my lisping Housemaster.

A few of the other Sixth Formers had managed to equip themselves with girl friends of a sort in the local town of St Austell, although this was one of the few things that were really illegal. They used to pant off on their bicycles, usually with civilian clothes in their saddle bags so that they could change out of the black school fancy dress, and mingle unnoticed with other cinema and pub goers. They would come back with lurid tales of things that they had learned about female physiology which held the stay-at-homes spellbound.

14

My normal route to school from Granham was on slow trains with changes at Bath, Bristol and Plymouth, and finally to Par. From the age of thirteen or so, I was accustomed to making this heroic journey on my own. At the beginning of one term, I had to crunch over the broken glass on foot through the badly-damaged city centre of Bath, the line through the town having been wrecked by a raid the previous night, and on subsequent journeys the same thing happened separately in both Bristol and Plymouth. Sometimes it seemed as if the Germans were bent on severing the lines of communication to my penitentiary. Then it went quiet for months, although at Marlborough during the holidays we exulted as ever-increasing RAF aerial armadas blacked out the moon as they thundered down to their rallying point near Southampton, and the wings of the tightly formated Flying Fortresses glinted high up in the sun as they kept up the pressure by day.

Then the signs of war in Cornwall reached another crescendo in early 1944. We watched a black Heinkel leisurely circling and bombing the Charlestown iron works, just over a mile away – a rather poor use of the Führer's precious arms and hydrocarbons because it was an innocent little place – while scattered soldiery fired their rifles at it. I felt tempted to pull out my pocket Derringer and send a lead slug whistling westwards into the sky after it, but decided regretfully that it was out of range, whilst various more immediately dangerous enemies like schoolmasters were definitely within range.

A few days later, some boys standing on the clifftop waved to a fighter aircraft passing at their level fifty feet away, then realized as the pilot waved cheerily back that it was a Messerschmitt 109F. But these events were only appetizers.

Suddenly, armies of Americans began to stream into tented camps north of us to practise for the invasion, which we all knew could not be long delayed. DUKW amphibious lorries plodded out into the bay to learn loading techniques moored against the rusty sides of freighters anchored there for the purpose. Amphibious tanks with mine-destroying gantries of chains at the front, thrashed up and down the rough beach letting off practice charges. The clatter of machine guns and rifles echoed continuously round the bay, along with the whoosh of bazookas and the thud of Piat anti-tank missiles. And there were languid, expensively-dressed American soldiers everywhere, whose easy manners and glamorous accoutrements stole the hearts of the local maidens, so that our feeble efforts to enjoy female company became even more unavailing.

A battalion of Gurkhas moved in as well, and began carrying out exercises in climbing the rugged cliffs leading their mules. The wonderful indestructibility of these saturnine little men was well demonstrated to us one day when, arriving with great difficulty at a point just below the top of the cliff, a mule and its master lost their footing. They bumped and rolled 150 feet down the steep rock face all the way to the bottom. Stationary at last, the little soldier jumped smartly to his feet and saluted apologetically to the officer in charge, but the mule did not move.

We had all accepted that some of the senior boys would leave the school and disappear for ever, and this began happening with increasing frequency. We had at King's in those days a system of fagging, something which has now vanished from all schools. In our case, for our first three terms, we were attached as sort of batmen to monitors in our own House, and they could and did demand menial services, including shoe-cleaning, the sweeping out of the studies, the making of their beds, and the preparing of tea. Sometimes the practice was abused, and thirteen-year-old boys felt like downtrodden lackeys much of the time.

I had three different fagmasters in my three terms, and two of them were killed within months of leaving school. G. A. H. Baker was in the Guards Chapel near Buckingham Palace when 200 officers and men were killed by a flying bomb, and I understand that J. D. Armstrong died on the bridge of a ship under attack in the South Pacific. It did not seem to put us off looking forward with impatience and envy to the time when we could go and risk our lives as well. I had no doubt that I wanted to be a Spitfire pilot.

The occupying American Army disappeared as abruptly as it had come, men and ships streaming out one evening across the Channel for what must ever remain one of the most unselfishly heroic days in the history of mankind. One of the best organized, too. We were sorry to see our new found friends go. They had also swarmed round Granham in the holidays, and I had thoroughly enjoyed their strength, friendliness and competence when lads from Oklahoma and Kansas had insisted on helping on the farm behind our house in their spare time.

For a time, it seemed that we could hear the distant rumble of guns in the Cherbourg Peninsula, then the sound retreated. Nowadays we tend to think that the invasion was bound to succeed because it involved such overwhelming might and such superhuman planning, but at the time it seemed anything but a foregone conclusion. The weather was so awful – perched on the clifftop as our hotel was, we felt every knot of gales like the one that sprang up just after the ships had sailed off on June 5th. But, once the bitter Ardennes offensive had come and gone in the Christmas of 1944, we knew that we would soon be heading away from Mevagissey, St Blazey Gate and Menabilly in our Cornish adventure playground, and back to the relative dullness of Kent.

Then, suddenly, my parents reappeared from Africa. I had not seen them for nearly six years, and now I stood five foot ten inches and towered over them. My father had developed an eye affliction, which seemed at one time likely to make him blind, and the Colonial Office had invalided him home. He came back, glad enough to see his children, and amazed at what big and self-possessed creatures they had become; whilst at the same time saddened at the thought that he was leaving behind him his life's work, the birds of East Africa.

I found them a bed-and-breakfast house in St Blazey, not far from the school, and they stayed there for some weeks while we got to know one another again. We had more in common than some families do. I had maintained my interest in wild flowers, started as a hobby by my mother on 'explorey' walks in our extreme youth. My father was a good linguist, which appealed to me. He could manage quite a lot of French, Spanish and German, in addition to excellent Arabic and Swahili. We liked maps, and wandering round using them on foot, bicycle and car. We were all hugely interested in our environment, whether marine biology, sunsets, waterfalls or fossils. And we were all fascinated by people, particularly if they showed the gorgeous elements of eccentricity that so many of our friends and relatives had manifested in the past. On the other hand, there were large areas of my own interests which were quite beyond them. I was drawn by all kinds of vehicles, from tractors up, and dreamed of flying aeroplanes one day quite soon. I still fired any kind of weapon whenever I could get my trigger finger on it, and let off home-made hand grenades. I practised vigorous sports, such as running the half mile, throwing the javelin, and doing the long jump. And I had begun to fantasize about girls with the same intensity as men dying of thirst in the desert think of laughing mountain springs.

Meanwhile, my redoubtable sister had gone from working as a seventeen-year-old Landgirl in a Wiltshire village called Oare, to being flying controller in the WRNS. Among her responsibilities there had been looking after thirty or so Guernsey cows, and because one of her charges was called Prinia after her, this exclusive name found its way into the *Guernsey Herd Book*. In due course, a large white pig was also officially named after her.

She began to collect amazingly glamorous Fleet Air Arm boyfriends, hung about with Wings, every available campaign medal, and quite a few gallantry ones. I watched her postings to active service aerodromes with envy.

Aged sixteen, I had also lost my heart twice in rapid succession. It was surprising to note how correct were the clinical details of the condition as described in the stories printed in a sloppy religious magazine called *The Quiver* to which our guardian subscribed. I well remember going off my morning porridge – and indeed the rest of my food – for days on end, and cycling aimlessly about in the broad main street of Marlborough, hoping to catch a quick glimpse of one or other of the beloveds. One of them wrote to me at school, and the first time, because she had only heard my name pronounced once, it came out as Morhgue on the envelope. Blushing scarlet as it was held up for claimants, I recognized the wildly sloping handwriting immediately, and tore the envelope open with trembling hands.

Meanwhile, Miss Jeans' lease at our beloved Granham had run out, and she had moved further west in Wiltshire to a tiny village almost on the border of Somerset. My parents and I retired there in the holidays, along with the Lawrences, mother and son, Lady Fowler of the Antiphlogiston incidents, Billy, and a few old ladies.

Chicklade was the name of the new village. I had by then read *Cold Comfort Farm*, and it reminded me almost irresistibly of the village of Howling in that unpredictable work. Since our only means of transport in those rationed days was our bicycles, and there was little to do apart from ornithology and gardening, my father and I did a lot of volunteer harvest work there for the bronchitic Mr Garland who lived opposite, and for a permanently-smiling farmer called Ollie Stevens. He was from an ancient Wiltshire family of yeomen, dark, short and extraordinarily muscular, like the Celts that lived in the local earthwork castles and pit villages on the chalk downs three thousand years ago. When Ollie swung the starting handle of a Fordson tractor, the whole ton and a half of it rocked wildly from side to side, paraffin slopping in its tank. It would not have dared to refuse to splutter into life. An eighteen stone sack of wheat would be tossed over his shoulder as if it were a feather pillow. And, once, I saw him climb a ladder up a rick with two hundredweight of folded tarpaulin on his head.

Olive Jeans' new guest house nestled up against the church, and, indeed, it was the old rectory. It was very convenient for frequent religious exercises, and Miss Jeans was let loose on another harmonium motheaten by time. I was paid a small sum as before to devastate the large garden and chop down unwanted trees. But it was not long before I got into trouble, as usual.

The airborne forces had been rehearsing for various forays into occupied Europe, including Arnhem. With their usual thoroughness, up on the heavily wooded down between us and

Wylye seven miles away, they had laid out a rather murderous obstacle course of anti-personnel mines, as noisy, if not as lethal, as the sort that they would be likely to meet in their real battles.

Late one afternoon, cycling aimlessly up a long hill towards the descent into Wylye, I saw markings on the bushes on my left that indicated that it was the beginning of one of the practice courses. I laid my bike down on the grass by the road, and began a reconnaissance. The track was marked with white tape on both sides to lull unsuspecting warriors into a false state of security, but I could also see that there were thin trip wires stretched across the fairway. Cautiously, I stepped my way over them, moving very slowly. Looking a little closer at one of the detonators intended to set off the booby traps that were hidden behind the stems of the trees, I saw that it consisted of a gunmetal trigger device containing a .38 cartridge, with a short length of instantaneous fuse leading to the actual bomb. My usual acquisitiveness about lethal hardware asserted itself.

'If I cut the fuse before trying to liberate one of the triggers,' I reasoned, 'then, even if I accidentally let off one of the cartridges, the bang should be pretty harmless.'

I always carried a pair of scissors in the toolkit round my waist, and now I drew them. Handling the detonator with the same gingerliness that I had always used when mixing up my favourite explosive in the lab, I was just about to start sawing at the orange fuse with the blades, when there was the most tremendous explosion inches in front of me. I heard bits crashing off through the bushes, and several seemed to collide with me. One piece hit me in the right eye, which may be the reason that it does not always work very well. And another splinter seemed to half-sever the middle finger on my right hand.

I was only semiconscious, and could see nothing through my right eye, and rather less than usual through my left one. My clothing had been blackened and torn, and my then thick hair had been badly singed. Although I did not feel lucky at the time, in fact, I had been, because the full force of the explosion had been directed away from me by the tree bole, otherwise I should not be writing this forty-five years later.

I considered the position for a minute or two, sitting on my hunkers. I had first of all to extract myself from the assault course, and half-blinded, it was not going to be so easy to avoid blundering into more trip wires, and doing the job properly. Also, I seemed to be leaking blood in a rather untidy fashion, and I might not be able to do that for very long without feeling a bit odd.

Squinting through my good eye, which was slowly recovering from the effects of the huge flash at close range, I inched my way back to the roadside. In those days, apart from the tanks and armoured cars that abounded on Salisbury Plain, there was very little civilian traffic, and it was quite clear that I could only abandon my bicycle under a bush and hope that one day soon I would be able to come back for it. So, singed, smoke-blackened and full of metal splinters, I stood forlornly at the side of the road, thumbing a lift.

By sheer luck, a kindly old man was driving past in an Austin Ten. I half-fell into his back seat, and proceeded to bleed all over his cushions, while his equally nice wife fussed over me.

The luck continued; he knew the excellent London eye surgeon who came down to Tisbury for week-ends – it was a Saturday – and within a quarter of an hour I was sitting in his small surgery while he extracted the splinter from my cornea with exquisite delicacy. I had already thought uneasily during the journey of the unpleasant stories that I had heard about damaged eyes being plucked out to avoid them destroying the good ones with anti-eye antibodies.

My parents had, of course, been unaware of all these dramas, and the first that they knew of it was when my elderly benefactor delivered me back to the Old Rectory, and I staggered in like a Shakespearian Bloody Captain. I was consigned to bed while my middle finger joined itself back on to the rest of me, and my eye learned to focus through its scars. I had not had so much attention for a long time.

As soon as I could write again, I penned another letter to the War Office, hoping that it would not end up again with H. Brown, Major. In it, I pointed out that His Majesty's Forces had left some dangerous weapons unattended in a public place, contrary to good order and discipline, and, with the natural curiosity of guileless children (I was just seventeen) I had fingered one of them, and consequently blown myself up. I considered that I might never be the same carefree, perfectly co-ordinated specimen again.

It says something for the Compensation Department of the War House that, while Typhoons were plunging into the ground among the milling German tanks in the Falaise Gap, and the fate of the Western Armies hung in the balance, they managed to send me an ex-gratia payment of £30 in full and final settlement, with a rider that I would not be so lucky again if I tinkered with battlefield left-overs. The money came in very useful a few years later when I bought my first motor cycle.

15

My daily reading of the *Daily Mirror* had given me a restricted picture to date of the German nation. They were generally seen scowling lethally under coal-scuttle helmets; manning shrieking Stuka bombers as they pitched vertically down on lines of overburdened refugees; or crowding as parachutists onto JU52 troop carriers – apparently made of corrugated iron – ready to rain down on defenceless countries from Holland to Crete.

Now that Burnwell had obliged me to learn German with all speed, I discovered a new, kindlier Teutonic world. The particular book that I chose for my solitary study was full of cosy little poems about fountains rustling like ripe corn in the night-time cobbled squares in South Germany, and of hearty blond students who strode singing from one hospitable village to the next during their *Wanderjahre*.

Hans Carossa gave me a sunny picture of life as a general practitioner in the broad meadows of Upper Bavaria, still haunted by the grandiose spirit of the castle builder Ludwig the Mad. E. T. A. Hoffman showed me the world of German whimsy, in which the Archivarius Lindhorst toured about the skies disguised at a giant raptor, and sweet little golden snakes with blue eyes writhed about.

I even warmed to Goethe, who, according to my book, expired in 1832 shouting 'More light, more light.' This was mainly because the early chapters of his autobiography *Dichtung und Wahrheit* described lovingly his affair with Frederika while he was an undergraduate at Strasbourg, and I effortlessly identified Frederika as one of my early amours.

I had taken on a substantial task in trying to learn German up to A-Level in just over a year, particularly because, for obvious reasons, it was not possible to do what I have since done with other languages – immerse myself in the native society. As a substitute, I used to spot German POWs working on Cornish farms by the distinctive coloured patches that they wore let into the backs of their brown battledresses, and try to hold primitive conversations with them. I soon recognized that their country had a remarkable variety of accents and dialects, and tried wherever possible to imitate those that came from North Germany and the Rhineland.

I also listened to the German radio, which produced the laughable Anglo-Irish voice of Lord Haw-Haw, maundering on in an attempt to destabilise us. But there was also quite a lot of solid propaganda spoken in good *Deutscher Rundfunk* German.

To help me in saturating myself in German, I played harpsichord Bach fugues and cantatas on the gramophone in my study, economizing by using hawthorns instead of expensive metal needles. Recordings of German marching songs were understandably frowned upon, but someone lent me a scratchy record of them, and I enjoyed trying to pick out the words shouted by the virile voices.

I listened also to the speeches of Hitler, wondering how on earth a runt with black hair who shrieked his words in a near-castrato could have come to supervise the breeding experiments that were going to enable the tall blond Herrenvolk to dominate us for a thousand years.

Apart from rare classes with the excellent 'Peeny' Voigt, I had to study on my own because to meet my summer exam deadline it was essential to move far faster through the language than any class attempted.

I have, as it happens, always found that the droning of a teacher is largely a distraction in the learning process, and, if I wish to absorb a mass of information in a short time, the only way is to sweat it out alone with a book. It is rare that any don or professor can provide additional information, and the sound of the human voice is also compellingly sleep-inducing.

There was another advantage. Being unsupervised, I could get up to a number of pleasurable activities in working hours, such as slipping out on my trusty, rusty bicycle to one of the more inaccessible beaches to look for useful flotsam, or for a spot of rockpool analysis, the firing of a weapon from my growing arsenal in a suitable cave, or even the letting off of my latest mark of hand grenade. I could even go and blush and stammer my way through a conversation with a barmaid somewhere, although I had already discovered that beer was an unpleasant drink.

I found this out because one of my closest friends, Tony Payne, belonged to the family that owned the St Austell Brewery. On one occasion, we went round it, tasting the products of each department, and I bravely struggled through a bottle of strong ale – although it tasted as bitter as quinine – then flushed it down with a large bottle of sweet cider. I have a very blurred recollection of whizzing down the hills and through the narrow lanes of the three-mile return journey to Carlyon Bay.

Tony Payne was also a remarkable mimic, and could produce with hysterical realism noises such as the complex and inexorable flushing of an old fashioned lavatory. He invariably ornamented the bottom classes, and this *sotto voce* sound from the back was his main contribution to lessons.

Occasionally, I regretted that I had barred myself from medicine. My father had made a serious attempt to persuade me to continue with it by post from Africa. And he had arranged for me to go up to Cambridge to see W. H. (Bill) Thorpe, then an entomologist, but later to become Professor of Animal Behaviour. He met me in the blackout at Cambridge station, and wheeled my case three miles on his bicycle to his strange cubist house on the western outskirts of the town.

I remember telling him a few fibs when he was questioning me about the reasons for my decision: I had concluded, I said, that I might swoon at the sight of blood. Also, I had discovered belatedly that ill people made me feel rather eerie. And anyway, my masters had told me that I was too stupid to manage advanced physics and chemistry. I did not mention to this kindly and well-intentioned man that it was really just that I felt that I had won the last battle with Burnwell, and I was glad to leave it at that.

After the near-run-thing of the vicious German offensive in the Ardennes at Christmas 1944, it became clear at last that their economy and army were folding under the fearful pressure that the Allies were exerting, and that we schoolboys were not going to have the brief glory of being cannon fodder after all.

I passed my Higher Certificate, and at the same time, the decision was taken to move the school back to Canterbury. As one of the senior boys, I was asked to parade back at the Kent end before the beginning of the next term to help to get things straight. Arriving there, I found that the Headmaster had been sufficiently moved by my exam result to promote me to school monitor on the field of battle. Having devoted myself for so long to serious misdemeanours, I realized that quite a lot of re-thinking would be necessary to become an upright citizen.

Before I left Carlyon Bay for the last time, I wandered about saying goodbye in a pantheistic mood that would have delighted Wordsworth. After five years there, I found many things highly nostalgic. There was, for example, the chuffing of the steam engine that pumped hot water to the farthest reaches of the big, ugly building. This echoed up from the great cellars, univers-ally known as 'the Maginot Line'. The pump was tended day and night by a sadly deformed man known as the 'Triangular Boilerman', who, oilcan in hand, dodged about among the jets of steam like a demon. The Maginot Line also housed the long room in which the school monitors carried out their ceremonial beatings, and, above the puffing of the steam engines, we could often hear the savage cracks of boys' bottoms being bruised.

In front of the hotel and between the garden and the vertiginous edge of the cliff lay a few yards of rough turf. One evening, an unstable scholar who, legend claimed, abused himself up to fifteen times a day, suddenly leapt up from his prep time desk, shouted, 'I can't take it any more,' crashed out through the door, and raced for the cliff. His intention was clearly to throw himself over, and into whatever hereafter is reserved for despairing onanists. Just before he reached the gorsebushes that marked the lip, he was brought down by a flying rugger tackle from a stalwart scrum player called I. K. Meeke, so that he lived to gratify himself another day. But the opportunity for generating further anxiety in us was not missed by pointing out that this was yet another side effect of the Awful Activity, to be put alongside others such as growing hair on the palms of our hands, and developing pitifully short sight.

In the latter days of the war, I had become a sergeant in the Junior Training Corps, wearing also the red badge of the fearsome-sounding War Certificate A. I developed a very loud parade-ground voice, and marched my platoon to and from with a martinet's attention to arm-swinging and keeping in step. One of the gangling youths under my command subsequently became an important millionaire in the car industry, another developed into one of London's best-known croupiers, and a third ultimately reached the rank of lieutenant-general in the British Army. I like to think that the qualities of manliness instilled by my square-bashing helped them to reach these dizzy heights.

We used to have mock battles up and down Black Head and Menabilly Peninsula, in which thunderflashes were popped hissing into one another's trouser pockets, and blank rounds were fired at the unwary close enough to singe our khaki uniforms. These battledresses were steeped in some whitish solution which we were told was to discourage infestation by lice in the field – about the only hazard which eluded us – and this produced an even stranger smell when burnt by cordite or a thunderflash.

Mock battles were always an excuse for the most tremendous frolics. Sometimes whole platoons would disappear in pursuit of a reported couple of sunbathing girls, or roadblocks would be set up and a ransom of cigarettes or sixpences demanded from disgruntled drivers. Pathetic-looking boy soldiers would hang round cakeshops until the motherly staff took pity on them. Stones would be dropped down abandoned tin mines so that we could measure the depth by counting our heart beats until the subterranean splash. And, in the midst of this shambles, Captain Eggy-Whistle and Sergeant Major 'Barch' Marshall would calmly continue refereeing as if the battle was going as reassuringly as that on the bloodless, untrodden snow at Hohenlinden.

The balmy Cornish Riviera, land of hydrangeas, palm trees and boyish adventures, seemed very hard to leave, but finally several special trains puffed out of Par Station heaped with our battered impedimenta, and we were on our way back to the chill winds and regimentation of Canterbury.

There, mysterious things happened to me. I have already mentioned my unexpected role as a School Monitor, with the right to wear a full length purple gown, thrash people, carry a walking stick, have all my coat buttons undone and my collar turned up, and other bizarre privileges too numerous to mention. And I was also asked which of the various school societies made defunct by evacuation I would like to restart as chairman or president.

Because of my love of discharging firearms, I opted to be Captain of Shooting, and also, for different reasons, to be President of the Debating Society. I chose the latter because at the time the thought of speaking unrehearsed in public made me shrink with horror. And it occurred to me that the only way of avoiding being asked to attack or defend motions would be to head up the whole operation. In various roles since then I have found this a useful way of shirking distasteful tasks, or those in which I would expect to fail.

I chose a third role as well; Officer-in-Charge of the Chapter House. This fine barrel-vaulted chamber was used by the school while the chapel was being re-built, and I had to keep it orderly. But the key that fitted it also let me in to the whole of the rest of the Cathedral, and I used to prowl round the clerestory and triforium in the dark, disturbing the bats, and listening to the deafening creaking of the rood screen and pews in the choir.

My second in command in the Shooting Eight was Tom Pares, who nowadays would be called a Young Fogey. He used to talk proudly of his father's achievements on the golf course, notably of the time when, considering that his performance in a match had been below par, he pulled each of his clubs separately out of the bag and broke them over his knee when he got back to the clubhouse. Tom's cousin, Alistair Walter Arthur Ernest Kneller, was the Captain of School. It was clear that his eloquence and man management abilities would qualify him in due course for high office, and I understand that he is now Lord Chief Justice of Gibraltar.

The school, under the shadow of the Cathedral, was a barely habitable shambles when we got back to it. The Germans decided quite early in the war that it would be bad for British morale if they bombed everything in Southern England which merited three stars in their Baedeker Guides.

On this basis, one of the succulent targets qualifying was Canterbury Cathedral, started by St Augustine along with the school in AD 603. Unfortunately for them, their marksmanship was not up to the standard of their excellent Guides, and almost all the bombs missed the 502 foot long edifice, and crashed on auxiliary buildings, such as the Cathedral Library, Deanery, school library and School House.

The big Green Court in the centre of the school had been excavated for air raid shelters, and also cabbage patches, where the occupants Dug for Victory between raids. The new classrooms and the School Hall were still being built. We slept, worked and played on a giant building site, smelling of drying concrete and new paint, accustoming ourselves slowly to the big dose of ecclestiasticism that resulted from the proximity of this major Mother Church. The chain-smoking Archbishop Fisher had died shortly before, and been succeeded by the more likeable William Temple, who was quite often seen about in the Precincts, beaming affably above one of his recently laundered bell tents.

Another figure that we saw frequently was the nationally famous Red Dean, Hewlett Johnson, who sported a highly polished bald pate between efflorescences of white hair that covered his ears. He had an uncompromising love of Communism and Stalin's Russia. From the pulpit, during one of his curiously interesting sermons, I once heard him say that, on his many visits to the Soviet Union, he had never once seen anything that he would not have wished an innocent sixteen-year-old girl to have seen with him. Considering, with the useful hindsight that history gives, that about this time Stalin was busy with a record massacre of nearly ten million people, it makes you realise how carefully this distinguished prelate's many trips to Russia must have been stage-managed.

He was not, however, without an extraordinarily kind streak of Christian Socialism, of which the following is an example. Years after my time in Canterbury, Professor E. C. Amoroso, who occupied the Chair of Animal Physiology at the Royal Veterinary College for a quarter of a century, and also held Fellowships in human medicine as a surgeon, obstetrician, gynaecologist, and physician, told me how he started his glittering academic career.

105

As a coloured student from Trinidad, he had battled his way through the medical course at Trinity College, Dublin, and finally qualified as a doctor. Life was hard for coloured men and women in British professions between the wars, and he had several humiliating experiences when applying for the medical research posts that he longed to fill. The only jobs in medicine that he could scrape were as a locum in practices round the country where a GP was temporarily absent. One day, travelling miserably back to a temporary post in Dover after a weekend in London, he noticed that the large, distinguished-looking cleric sitting opposite him was reading, of all things, a copy of the *New Scientist*.

Their eyes met, and the Red Dean said suddenly to the depressed young doctor, 'Something's troubling you, young man. Can I help?'

'Amo' (as he was subsequently called by generations of students, and the medical community throughout the world) explained with tears in his eyes how he had longed to devote his life to medical research, but no one would help him because of his origins. The Red Dean listened sympathetically, then, when Amo had finished, said, 'When the train stops at Canterbury, you come along with me. You can stay the night in the Deanery, then in the morning I'll ring the Director of the Royal Veterinary College. I see from this journal that he has a job going as a reader/demonstrator. I'm sure that I can get it for you.' He was as good as his word, and Amo rewarded him over the years by making a huge contribution to endocrinology and veterinary science.

When the repairs to the old library had been completed, King George VI, Queen Elizabeth and Princess Elizabeth – freshly out of the ATS – came down to open it. At the time, my only experience of Royalty had been meeting the Duke of Kent for twenty seconds when he drove down in a sports Bentley to see us in Cornwall. I remembered him arriving on the hotel forecourt, abundant evidence of the speed at which he had driven being provided by thick fly squash on the windscreen. In the back sat a husky bodyguard, a loaded Tommy Gun across his knees.

The Monarchs did not arrive in such a heroic fashion. The

106

King was in a perfectly tailored Naval uniform, his face so highly coloured that it looked as if he was wearing make-up. Queen Elizabeth – now the Queen Mother – was her usual homely, forthcoming self in powder blue. It was my first experience of trying to entertain the impossibly famous, and I found the pressure of their status and renown almost overwhelming until the King, having asked me what I was going to do next, suddenly boomed without a trace of a stammer, 'Can't think what the ruddy Government thinks it's doing, still forcing young chaps like you into the Army, now that we've won the war.'

This glimpse of a man who disagreed with his own Government was so endearing that we all relaxed immediately. One or two brave souls even tried to chat up Princess Elizabeth, but she wasn't having any. I am sure that by then she had lost her heart to her bemedalled sailor Prince, and all these fresh-faced, long-haired nothings in their stiff wing collars and black suits seemed pretty small beer by comparison.

Meanwhile, former masters had been coming back from the war, bronzed, authoritative and decades younger than the dugouts who had previously taught us. One, who had emerged from the war as an RAF Wing Commander with a dazzling combat record in fighters, drove into the Mint Yard in a British Racing Green 3 litre vintage Bentley, which nicely completed his presentation. Then he spoiled it all for us by announcing that he was going into the Church. John Corner came back after a long war spent in the Intelligence Corps. One of the few regrets of my life is that he did his best to arrange a commission for me in his own Corps. But, when the moment came to choose my service at my military medical, I was seduced by my irresistible urge to fly, and opted for the RAF I could not have realised at the time that my dream of flying Spitfires was about to fall to pieces with the explosive contraction to a peacetime Service.

Finally, the moment came to leave. As before, I had outgrown the ethos of school, and it was with a sigh of relief that I caught the train away from Canterbury and into the world of grown-ups.

16

My parents had now gone to stay with Eric Mellor, a marvellous old eccentric who had often gone on safari with them in their Egyptian days. He quite unselfconsciously told me that his mother, bored out of her mind by her English husband, had gone to play the tables at Biarritz in the 1890s. Meeting the limpid brown eyes of a dashing French aristocrat across the smoke-shrouded baccarat table, she yielded to him shortly afterwards in a brief but steamy affair. Eric Mellor was the result, and he put down to the Gallic moiety of his personality his love for berets, the French language, its history and its cuisine.

It was not only for this reason that he appealed to me. He also told how one day in the Egyptian desert on the way to Alexandria, he saw a train chuffing over the dunes in a straight line at right angles to him. Knowing that there was an unguarded level crossing ahead, and being a sporting man, he accelerated along the dusty track to race it there. Unfortunately, he had misjudged the train's speed in the shimmering air, and he spent several months in hospital after being hit amidships.

The house we all stayed in clung to the northernmost end of the Black Mountains, just where the road begins to labour up out of Bredwardine towards the hill village of Dorstone. The Wye rushed under the bridge below us, teeming with fish including salmon, and Mellor also kept a falcon, with which he was an expert. On his cellar door, appropriately for a *bon viveur* living in Herefordshire, he had some verses by Evoe that originally appeared in *Punch*. I thought that they showed a rare level of poetic craft, and also evoked a most lovable county, so I learned them by heart. They were based on a rather foolish pronouncement by the then Bishop of Hereford that 'there is much secret cider drinking in Herefordshire':

The wild white rose is cankered,
Along the vale of Lugg,
There's poison in the tankard,
There's murder in the mug.

Through all the pleasant valleys,
Where stand the pale-faced kine,
Men raise the Devil's chalice,
And drink his bitter wine.

In spite of Church or Chapel,
Ungodly folk there be,
Who pluck the cider apple,
From the cider apple tree.

And squeeze it in their presses,
Until the juice runs out,
At various addresses,
That no one knows about.

But still if strength suffices,
Before my day is done,
I'll go and share the vices,
Of Clungunford and Clun.

And watch the red sun sinking,
Across the March again,
And join the secret drinking,
Of outlaws at Presteigne.

Unspeakable carouses,
That shame the summer sky,
Take place in little houses,
That look toward the Wye.

And near the Radnor border,
And the dark hills of Wales,
Beelzebub is warden,
And sorcery prevails.

And maddened by the orgies,
Of that unholy brew,
They slit each others' gorges,
From 1 a.m. till 2.

Till Ledbury is a shambles,
And in the dirt and mud,
Where Leominster sits and gambles,
The dice are stained with blood.

As usual I had brought my ancient, heavy-framed bicycle with me, and what was left of the three speed gearing did yeoman service on the exhausting hills of the area. One of my favourite rides was southwards out of Hay-on-Wye, and up over the rough, sheep-grazed moorland to the pass that led to Capel y Ffin. I used to abandon my bike at the edge of the stony track at the top, and climb to the 2200 foot summit of Lord Hereford's Knob, with its luminous view over to Clyro – where the Reverend Francis Kilvert wrote his diaries between 1840 and 1879 – and the massive hulk of the Brecon Beacons. It always seemed to me very appropriate that the icthyphallic Eric Gill ran his weird sect in a colony under the shadow of such a quaintly named mountain.

At this time, I acquired a taste for the Black Mountains which has remained with me. The Alpine ranges which I have spent so much time in since are higher and more inaccessible, and more often snow-clad; but there is something about the sunlit remoteness of these grassy green bastions to Wales which is irresistible. Only eight miles across at its widest point, it seems like a land which time has completely passed by. And there are buildings of remarkable antiquity to explore, such as Llanthony Abbey, and, nowadays, the remarkable network of caves and passages discovered in 1966.

Through necessity and constitutional meanness with myself, I have always managed to make a small amount of money go a long way, and the shillings that I earned with various gardening, harvesting and Post Office jobs could usually be managed so frugally that I probably seemed somewhat less pitifully poor than I in fact was. Now, because my father had been retired early on a reduced pension, and I no longer justified a penny of pocket money, it was rapidly obvious that I must get a job pending being called up to serve the King.

I knew that there was an agricultural camp at Redhill on the edge of Hereford town, and, after a week or two in Mellor's cottage at Bredwardine, I moved there to live in. The work was very hard. I spent hours up ladders every day picking apples and other fruit, and learned to perform aerial manoeuvres twenty feet up that have stood me in good stead ever since. We also culled everything else – raspberries, blackcurrants, plums, potatoes, and so on. But really, the day's work, and the pound or so that we earned each day, were only prologues to the real activity of the camp: sex. As a consequence of the isolation that public schoolboys used to suffer, often in the holidays as well, I felt that I had a lot of leeway to make up, and the camp provided an ideal opportunity.

I shared a room with a lance-corporal on leave from the Army of Occupation in Germany. In those days, according to him, a packet of Wills Woodbine cigarettes would buy you the favours of a whole roomful of Fräuleins. Licking his lips, he would show me one photo after another of his busty German conquests, some of whom were in striking unclad postures. We had a pretty vivid few weeks because he thought that similar techniques based on giving away cigarettes and chocolate would destroy the resistance of the sturdy British girl students in the camp. Sometimes I would be already in bed, exhausted by the effort of working a twenty-foot ladder round tree after tree without descending to the ground, when Mick would come in with an unwilling bit of totty. In the darkness, there would be a lot of stertorously heavy breathing, ending in a few grunts and cries of 'Stop it!', followed by a door-slamming withdrawal, and mutterings of disappointment from my room mate.

Because of these reverses, I delayed for a bit my first foray into the art of gaining consent. Out in the shadows near the wire that surrounded the camp with a healthily pneumatic girl called Rita, I had just began to palpate some areas of marshmallow succulence, when she too remembered an urgent engagement elsewhere. Then I discovered the warm-hearted school-mistresses who abounded in the huts of the female ghetto, and

111

swiftly realized why bundling was such a much-esteemed export from beyond the Marches.

Meanwhile, my sister had been demobilized from the WRNS after her gallant war service in Flying Control. She arrived with a leggy friend called Margaret Birtwhistle, and got stuck into the hard work with the energy and strength that you would expect from an ex-Land Girl. She introduced me to her normal form of transport – hitchhiking. She went on to develop it into an art form, travelling across Europe on her own, sleeping in holes in the sand on French beaches. I got bitten by the bug as well, and for the next five years saved hundreds of pounds of fares thanks to the hospitality of lorry drivers and family motorists, at home and abroad.

I also made a lot of friends by this form of travel. One of the most charming was an elderly Deputy Headmaster in Merthyr Tydfil called Mordecai Evans. Toiling up the long hill out of that town one day, pack on my back, no one would stop for me, so I asked this dignified green-eyed gentleman if he could tell me anything about the public transport on that road. His response was to usher me on to a bus which shortly passed, and sit with me all the way to Tredegar, insisting on giving me money for the journey on. Months later, I sent this modest sum back, only to have my money returned and doubled. We remained dear friends until his death many years later. He had a capacity for warmth and friendship given to few.

While I was at Redhill Camp, I submitted myself to a Service medical in Hereford town. To my great surprise in those days, I was declared A1 by a young and pretty woman doctor, who had earlier brought a flush to my cheeks by manually confirming the presence of my full complement of assets.

Still elated by this experience, I went into the room where the recruiting officers of the three Services sat smiling winsomely at their separate desks. As I mentioned earlier, I was struck between the eyes by the overt glamour of the Squadron Leader who sat there with two rows of gallantry and campaign medals, and even the tiny gold larva of the Caterpillar Club sprawled across one of the ribbons, the whole fruit salad topped by his gleaming wings. I went on to automatic pilot immediately, passed the young major who was going to help me into John

Corner's Intelligence Corps unit, and sat down starry-eyed like one of the lads from 'The Boyhood of Raleigh' in the Squadron Leader's chair. I shall never know what I missed in the I. Corps.

A few weeks later, I got my calling-up papers, and cutting my belongings down to the irreducible minimum as requested, I boarded a train for the square-bashing camp at Padgate, outside Warrington, known and feared by tens of thousands of airmen.

Recruit camps breed a curious type of NCO. Redeemed by their earthy humour which, unlike that of schoolmasters, is often hysterically funny, their behaviour is nevertheless almost wholly intended to diminish and dominate. It is hard to see how, geographically widely separated, they all learn to behave so uniformly. They have no equivalent in civilian life, except perhaps the occasional old-fashioned foreman, and trade union leaders like the now legendary Red Robbo.

The first event in my new existence as AC2 2326116, Moreau, D. M. was an intelligence test. Very sagaciously, the purpose of this was to help in assigning each of us to a trade. Many years before, the RAF had begun to believe in the doctrine favoured also, I believe, by Eysenck: that people are best able to cope with a particular or profession if they have IQs that correspond with the average of those already doing the job.

I must have been on my mettle that particular day, and scored so highly that I was told that becoming aircrew was not possible, and only one trade was open to me, that of Radar/Wireless mechanic. I pleaded, but they were adamant. My dream of becoming a steely-eyed throttle jockey was over for the time being.

The six weeks of rigorous square-bashing that followed are rather blurred in my memory, mainly because we were rooted out of bed at 6 a.m., which is not my best hour for consciousness. And, by the time that I woke properly at the end of the morning, I was already exhausted again by the mix of physical training, rifle drill, and doubling round the square. But in that time I noticed remarkable changes in the physiques of the frequently weedy lads that had been recruited from industrial towns. They put on a stone or two each of solid muscle and carried themselves quite differently.

Where the actual drilling was concerned, I had no difficulty, having already been a full-blown sergeant myself, but some of the other activities were different. We were paraded at the grenade range, for example, and hurled live Mills bombs across the devastated mud flats. I have never seen grown men so frightened as some of the recruits were. They went blue-green long before they were handed the attractively embossed little bombs, and the hands of some shook so badly that the corporal in charge had to take the pins out for them. Mind you, I quite understood their reaction. Although ripping explosions had been part of my daily life for years, the bang of a Mills bomb going off close to you is quite stunning. Also, we were told bloodcurdling stories about past events there before we even climbed into the wide throwing trenches.

One concerned a butterfingers of a recruit who had dropped a bomb beside him below the parapet. His life, and that of the other recruits had been saved by an infinitely gallant sergeant who had muffled the thing by lying down over it and eviscerating himself.

The time came for our prophylactic injections, universally known as 'jabs', ready to be sent overseas. A few weeks before I had cut a notice out of the Personal Column of *The Times*, which said that Servicemen should be aware that none of them could be forced to have an injection for anything unless they gave their specific consent. It was placed by some human rights organization.

When I was twelve years old, my school had forced me to have an injection against measles in my right buttock. Looking back, I think that it must have been an insufficiently attenuated live virus, and badly given into the sciatic nerve to boot, because not only did it paralyse my right leg for a week; it also gave me a thumping dose of measles.

That experience had cured me for ever of a belief in injected prophylaxis. I had concluded that the cure is usually worse than the disease, and I had resolved to refuse it in future.

The recruits queued quietly outside the MI room, mostly as pale as death once again. From inside, there was a steady thump of bodies slumping to the floor at the sight and feel of the gleaming needles, and soon the patch of grass outside was covered with recuperating airmen.

My turn came. The whole operation was being overseen by a medical Squadron Leader, his neck so fat that it was almost the same diameter as his head. I marched up to him, crashed up a smart salute, and said, 'Sir, I am requesting permission to refuse my jabs on the grounds of non-belief.'

He regarded me distastefully through his heavy spectacles.

'What did you say, Airman?' he barked intimidatingly.

'Sir, my conscience does not permit me to have injections,' I said, changing my ground a little.

He put his face dreadfully close to mine, and shouted 'You are prepared to risk the lives of your colleagues just because you are a coward, is that it?'

If I had not been brought up in a school where yelling masters threw themselves on you almost daily, my resistance would probably have collapsed at that point, and I would have bared my arm. As it was, I knew that, unlike Mr Bolingbroke, King's Regulations prohibited him from assaulting me, and mere verbal abuse would just bounce off.

'If I was a coward, Sir, I would not be saying this to you. I know my rights, and nothing you say will change my mind.' I had always wanted to say that about my rights to someone. To my great surprise, he said quietly: 'Right, Airman, fall in outside. And I hope I never have to treat you for any of these diseases.'

All the NCOs were aghast at my behaviour, and I quite expected to be treated as an outcast when I got back to my hut. Far from it. My comrades were all envious, and said so. And, when terrible vaccination reactions struck them the following day, I felt vindicated.

Shortly after this, because they saw me as a kamikaze where tangling with the officers was concerned, my Wing elected me to the Messing Complaints Committee, a sinecure, you might think, since little could be done to make more palatable the five basic elements that made up our daily diet – potatoes, sawdust sausages, cabbage, beans and suet stodge. But no. When I called for agenda items, an aggrieved little airman called AC Widgery arrived in my bedspace.

'It's that bugger of a messing officer,' he said bitterly, 'e's puttin' bloody yuge quantities of the bromide in our tea again.

115

We'll all be turnin' inter WAAFs next. You tell 'im it's got ter stop.'

So at the meeting that followed, I complained officially. As I finished, the CO who chaired it bared long equine teeth in shrill brays of laughter, but made no other comment. I reported this to AC Widgery. Incensed, he said, 'I'm warnin' yer. Ginger Smiff actually saw the messing officer puttin' cupfuls of green powder in our breakfast urns the other mornin'. We got the evidence now, it's up ter you to get some action while we're still men.'

Shortly afterwards, an Air Marshal's visit was announced, and we were all instructed to parade in the camp's vast corrugated iron cinema. We sat to attention through a series of rolling platitudes, then the Air Marshal stood up and called with slightly menacing avuncularity for any complaints. I hadn't planned anything, but suddenly realized that this was a first-class opportunity to get to the bottom of the bromide question.

A thousand faces veered dumbly towards me as I leapt to my feet, crying dramatically, 'Sir, into the Servot Multipots of 21 Group, a sinister poison is being dropped . . .'

'Speak up, airman,' bawled a flight sergeant. I had already discovered long ago at school that any interruptions of that sort were liable to destabilize me, and that was what happened on this occasion. The searing indictment which I had planned on the spur of the moment drained away through a mental plughole.

I staggered, mouthing, and steadied myself by grabbing the greasy curls of the airman next to me, before appealing round me: 'For God's sake, what was I saying?'

'Dunno, mate,' said someone boredly. I remembered an important word, and shouted it wildly: 'Servot Multipot.' Then AC Widgery came on faintly from the circle. 'You was tellin' 'im about the bromide, tosh,' he shouted.

I flickered briefly to life again. 'The bromide,' I half-screamed, 'thousands of sweethearts depend on it . . .' It went again.

'Is that airman trying to be funny?' said the Air Marshal testily. A flight sergeant was battling along the row towards me.

I had a last fling, 'We're all turning into WAAFs,' I snarled, then sat down with a bump before the flight sergeant could put the interlocutory half-nelson on me that he obviously had in mind. This incident further convinced me that public speaking was not my *métier*.

17

One day, while I was serving on number 94 Maintenance Unit near Thetford, an aircraftman called Kupinsky, who hailed from the Balls Pond Road, was marched before the CO. As a local, honorary and temporary Clerk General Duties, I was gravely noting the details to put in the airman's file.

As usual, the Station Flight sergeant recited the charges to the grave-looking Squadron Leader, who, in civilian life, had been a solicitor.

'I informed Aircraftman Kupinsky that 'e would be put on a charge,' he said heavily, 'on account of the fact that 'e was passin' water through the winder of 'is 'ut, contrary ter good order and discipline.' I sat transfixed in the corner, fighting with the desire to giggle.

Kupinsky defended himself vigorously: 'The toilets, airmen, was all occupied and I was taken short; the tea is too strong – or p'raps it's the bromide. Me bladder was weakened by the measles when I was a nipper. And, anyway, I thought that a drop of fertilizer might be good fer the lettuces growin' between the 'uts.' But, as with most service justice, the outcome was inevitable.

'A disgusting offence, Kupinsky,' said the CO primly, 'what would the camp be like in hot weather if we all adopted your repulsive solution? Seven days confined to camp, with extra cookhouse duties.'

'Thank you, sir,' said Kupinsky in the resigned manner of a survivor of aeons of pogroms.

'And wash your hands before you touch the airmen's food,' added the Squadron Leader, obviously struck suddenly by the thought that Kupinsky might try to repeat his exploits out of the potato room window.

When I first arrived at the cluster of huts in a pine forest, fresh from public school and a few weeks of training in the rebarbative north, it seemed to me that it was the sort of adventure camp that I had always yearned to live in. For example, the summer of 1946 had been quite steamy, and everyone talked longingly of building a swimming pool, without anyone in fact doing anything about it.

Then the Armaments Officer, an extremely bad-tempered Flight Lieutenant, solved the problem one afternoon. He took a group of Jamaicans on to a patch of waste land across the road, and stood over them while they dug a ten foot hole. Then, writing off as U/S one of the ugly-looking 500lb bombs stored in his department, he trollied it across the road, fused it carefully with a remotely-controlled detonator, lowered it down the excavation, and retired to a safe distance with a wire and plunger in his hand. Waiting for a gap in the passing traffic, he put a finger in one ear and sank the piston home. The blast wave broke a few windows in the guardroom at the gate, and the top of a fir tree sailed over onto the patch of gravel that did duty as a barrack square. But there was now a fine, clay-bottomed crater fifteen feet deep which a fatigue party was able to fill with a fire hose, while another group was set to tidying round the edges.

The camp existed for a curious reason. It housed a large proportion of the total British stockpile of chemical weapons, including phosgene and mustard gas, which the Services – and particularly the RAF – held in reserve in case Hitler ever let off anything similar. When the war ended, as it had only a matter of months before, the problem arose of how to rid ourselves safely of all those rusting cylinders, shrouded under curved corrugated iron sight screens.

The decision was taken to burn them. A workforce of airmen distinguished more by their stolid strength than their brain-power was assembled. And every day sections clad from head to foot in oilskins topped by gas masks marched into the area to drag out the gas cylinders and set fire to their contents, so that great oily clouds of pungent smoke drifted over the Norfolk countryside.

Although most of the camp's denizens looked like Neander-thalers in uniform, they needed their entertainment like any other Servicemen. Because of the danger and the extremely arduous work that was done, there were no WAAFs on the isolated camp at all, only one transvestite, who became the object of great concupiscence on camp dance nights. So on weekend nights as dusk fell the narrow road to Thetford was heavily trafficked by the boots of airmen. When I had just arrived, I naively asked the corporal on the gate where everyone was off to dressed in their best blues.

'They're after a bit of shuffle and grunt, mate,' he answered shortly, 'ain't nothing round 'ere 'cept bleeding sheep.' I found out later that only a tiny percentage of this lemming-like crowd were actually blessed by the girls of Thetford during the hunt for this much-esteemed commodity, but the men all nevertheless plodded into the silent main street of the little town past the flaring gasworks, to stand smoking in eager groups on the street corners waiting for something to happen, until it was time to walk back to camp again.

There were, however, other distractions. One was the station Fire Engine, a powerful Fordson. On warm summer evenings, an ex-bomber pilot, who was chronically carefree with the relief that came from surviving numerous trips through flak and fighters to such places as the marshalling yards at Hamm, used to parade a party of non-Shuffle and Grunters. They would cluster all over the rear of the vehicle, clutching Very pistols, and he would start off on a wild ride between the bomb huts. The idea was to take potshots at the game which abounds in that part of Norfolk; but, because accuracy is impossible with the arc-like trajectory of the heavy rocket, nobody ever hit anything. But a few hares and pheasants got the fright of their lives as red missiles thudded into the heather beside them. Usually, small fires started, which were delightedly put out by the now hysterical crew of the fire engine. They would usually continue this game until darkness fell, or their ammunition ran out.

There were two other distractions. On the east side of the camp, there was a huge entanglement of rusty barbed wire which, for some reason beyond science, could receive the Forces Network. Sometimes, a small, awed group of airmen would stand there as the strains of Victor Sylvester came eerily out of the darkness, produced, perhaps, by some ferric oxide crystals acting as a rectifier on the huge aerial of the entanglement. This being before the days of transistors, the supernatural amenity was much appreciated.

Leading Aircraftman Butcher was the other main entertainment. He owned an ancient, asthmatic Morris Eight with a dicky seat. When his petrol ration sufficed, he would take runs up a gravel path through the woods to an isolated pub maintained for the dozens of gamekeeping Tom Forrests in the locality. But the drive there was not an ordinary one.

Butcher himself, kneeling on the running board, would take the wheel. Three other airmen, crouching down headfirst, would take the clutch, brake and accelerator. And a noisy group in the dicky would lean forward and work the horn or the trafficators when the spirit moved them. The car would swerve and judder down the road, with Butcher shouting commands to the clutch and brakemen, most of which were ignored in the general uproar. The journey would be just survivable, provided that there was no other traffic on the track. But the trip back usually ended with excursions into the scenery, and a lot of drunken cheers as the car was heaved out of the ditch.

Of course, in those halcyon days, the Race Relations industry had not been invented, so that awful things were said daily to the various ethnic communities, usually only producing guffaws. One was in my own Orderly Room, a misnomer if ever there was one. The first day that I arrived, the Flight Sergeant asked me gruffly if I could read and write in a satisfactory manner. Not wishing to seem out of place in such a camp, I said, 'Yes, more or less.' and was then detailed off to join the other literates in the Administration.

Going shyly where I was posted, I asked each of my new colleagues his name. The only Jamaican in there, who was wearing a confection on his head that looked like a Melton Mowbray pie made by abusing his forage cap with an iron, said cheerily, 'Just call me the Black Bastard.'

'Oh, I couldn't do that,' I answered, rather shocked.

'Why not?' he said, creasing himself with hilarity, 'all the boys in here do. And, in any case, I am undeniably both black and a real bastard.'

As always, there were always a few troublemakers in the camp. One of them happened to be another Jamaican, nearly as big and strong as King Kong, and who expected to go to University and become a lawyer in his home island when he was demobilized. One day he complained to the Corporal of the Guard that his boots hurt – the Air Force had probably been unable to muster any size fourteens for him when he was kitted out. Rather unwisely, the corporal, relying on the tolerance that even the Irishmen in the camp showed, said, 'Well, when you buggers drop out of trees to join up, you can't expect to find it easy to wear white man's boots.' This was how the Jamaican came to find himself on a charge: 'That he did chase the Corporal of the Guard round the camp with a fire axe, contrary to good order and discipline.'

It took me a month or two to find my feet in the camp's nerve centre. But I matured with a bang after the Ration Card Affair. One morning, a telegram came in from the Air Ministry, requiring us to report by return how many airmen were currently on the camp so that suitable numbers of sweet and tobacco ration cards could be issued to us. I asked the Black Bastard how many we were, and he said, 'Tell them there are 850 of us here.'

'I can't tell them that, they must know already that that's about four times as many as we really are.'

He laughed his usual hysterical laugh.

'Don't be a rasklark, man,' he said, using a Jamaican word whose meaning I never discovered, 'dey haven't got a bloody clue up dere.'

So, in due course, we received a wildly excessive number of ration cards, which we all used in the succeeding months in the same way that prison barons use snout.

Shortly after this, another entertainment turned up, in the person of an AC called Abelberg, the son of a Harley Street psychiatrist. His time at a square-bashing camp had convinced him that life in the RAF was perfectly horrible, and he had resolved to work his way out, using what he believed to be a series of convincing psychiatric stratagems. After a few days of settling down, he turned up on the 8 a.m. morning parade wrapped in a colourful eiderdown, and wearing a yellow tulip behind his left ear.

The Flight Sergeant regarded him mockingly for a few

moments, then barked out, 'I should watch it with that flower, Abelberg. I just might get Kupinsky to water it.'

Abelberg, grimly determined to be a textbook case of dementia, stifled a smile, eyes flickering round the tittering ranks about him, and croaked, 'What flower, Flight Sergeant?' But the parade commander had made his one little joke, and now his temper was shortening.

'Go back to yer bloody 'ut, and leave yer sodding Granny's shawl and yer 'orticultural hadornments, or I'll put a fizzer on you fer insubordination,' he roared.

But Abelberg didn't give up. A series of other incidents took place, ending with his appearing in the flight office with motor oil all round his mouth, declaring that his anxiety as a highly strung person subjected to these military indignities had made him drink a pint of sump oil, taken from the ancient motor cycle and sidecar that he used to escape to London at weekends. He was sent to hospital to have his stomach pumped out, and a bit later duly got his discharge on psychiatric grounds.

Autumn and a golden Indian summer declined into winter at the camp, and suddenly quite a lot of the laughter died. It was the terrible January, February and March of 1947, and after all the lavatories and showers froze up, and coal for the hut stoves became short, we were all advised to go to bed in our uniforms to avoid hypothermia.

Even so, the outside of the bedclothes would be crackling with ice by the morning, the thin corrugated iron of the Nissen huts providing almost no insulation. Finally, the unbelievable happened. We were all sent home from a camp that had become uninhabitable. Stuffing our pockets with sweets and tobacco rations – the only luxury left – we climbed singing into the lorries, to struggle through the snowdrifts to civilization.

By now my parents had moved to Madingley, outside Cambridge, where they shared with a widow whose house was still haunted by the spirit of her dead husband. My father was being considered to head up the new department of Animal Behaviour in the University. Professor Tinbergen at Oxford was already making important contributions to this new study, originated by Lorenz in Germany, and destined to reach its

123

popular apotheosis much later in the not always admired hands of Desmond Morris.

My stay at Madingley was fairly short. Barnham camp finally unfroze, but I returned there only briefly, to embark on a lorry to travel down to RAF Yatesbury, at that time, the best university in the world in which to study modern airborne electronics.

It was like quitting the Old World, and entering an intellectual Promised Land. Not that the huts were very different. They were still made of creosoted planks, and the ablutions were still the standard cement-rendered issue, with a high, draughty, louvred section in the middle to let the steam out. And there was still a big barrack square, on which at Yatesbury stood the remains of a once proud Mosquito fighter, in process of being dismantled by aircraftman souvenir hunters.

But it was the quality of the hut occupants that made it so different. Every erk in the place had had to demonstrate an IQ in excess of 130 in order to get there at all, which in Oxbridge terms, would mean that anyone scoring less than a 2.1 in their Finals would not have been accepted for training. In both those universities, that would mean more than half of the current students. The consequence was a degree of eggheadness such as I have never encountered before or since, and many of my contemporary radar mechanics are now professors, or occupying top research positions throughout the country. Our universities would be very different places if equally high standards were demanded at entry.

Not that life at Yatesbury was dull or staid. I took a bet with an airman from Oxford that I would ride backwards on the pillion of his motor cycle all seven miles to Calne, while he tried to throw me off. About halfway there, I regretted my stupidity when I was deposited violently on the grass verge on my elbows, while he straightened up from his desperate swerves and rode triumphantly off.

We were also expert at imitating large beam steam engines. One man would plunge in and out in the vertical mode, representing the piston. Another would have his arms out-stretched as the beam, and a third would writhe his bottom round in circles as the flywheel. A fourth would stand making synchronised chuffing sounds. On one occasion, the Station Warrant officer marched smartly round the corner of the hut as we throbbed away, waiting for a class. He stopped short in amazement, then bawled,

'What the arseholes are you doing, airmen?'

The piston straightened up. 'We're explaining to our class-mate how a steam engine works, sir. It's part of the course.'

The Warrant Officer, who was only an ordinary general duties NCO, not a radar specialist, shifted from foot to foot. Staring at the piston's unshaking and reverential gaze, he made sure his mickey was not being pulled. Then, not being able to make a recognizable Air Force offence out of our antics, he just grunted and marched off.

One of the men in the next hut had been a stage hypnotist before being conscripted, and he used to hold demonstrations of his black arts most nights. His fellow airmen volunteered to have needles thrust through their unfeeling hands, arch their bodies between the backs of two chairs while the hypnotist sat on them, and undress and make exhibitions of themselves. But he was told to stop it after one of his subjects went into a trance during a lecture, and fell so deeply asleep that he had to be woken up in the sickbay.

One Friday afternoon, I happened to go into one of the classroom huts, and found a fellow student with the infinitely appropriate name of Mountjoy standing in front of the nozzles of a wave guide. This led from the magnetron of a large radar set, which was switched on. 'What on earth are you doing?' I asked, noting that the wave guide was pointing at his fly buttons.

'I'm going to see a new girl on a forty-eight hour pass tonight,' he said, 'and I don't want to put her in the family way, that's all.'

'How do you mean?' I asked in puzzlement.

'Well, I read in a scientific journal the other day that intense bombardment with microwave radiation kills sperm stone dead, causing temporary sterility. One of the corporal instructors told me he'd heard it too. So I'm giving it a go.'

After the weekend, I happened to see Mountjoy, limping down the road to his hut.

'What on earth's wrong with you?' I said.

'God knows,' he answered, 'all I can tell you is that it's taken a whole pot of Valderma to get my marriage gear back in working order.'

Nowadays, of course, any microwave owner could tell Mountjoy that the short waves had lightly boiled his parts.

18

During the radar course, which was claimed to reach inter-BSc standard, I became aware that electricity was not really my bag. Although I could soon intone V equals I over R with the best of them, I had difficulty with the concept of the watt as being work done at the rate of 10 to the power of 7 ergs per second. As everyone will remember, an erg is a unit of energy; it is the energy expended when a force of one dyne is exerted through one centimetre; and ten million dynes are equal to three-quarters of a foot/pound.

What bothered me most was that, since the wretched units were all interdependent, if you failed to understand one, your whole comprehension collapsed.

Thus, I sat staring uneasily at the definition of a volt as 'that e.m.f or p.d. which, when applied steadily to a conductor of resistance one ohm, produces a current of one ampere.' This, in turn, was because I had never really had a mental picture of the ludicrous unit invented by Andre Marie Ampere (1775–1836) – 'an ampere is that amount of current required to deposit 0.00118 grams of silver on the cathode of a silver voltameter in 1 second.' Can you imagine a DIY man cracking off a quick test for amperes like this in his workshop?

When I was at school, there was a boy called Taylor who had the most amazing grasp of radio technology. He was usually to be found alongside Tony Payne at the bottom of the most lowly class, but in a matter of minutes, he could construct a working radio for you out of paperclips, blotting paper, odd bits of wire and assorted scraps of waste metal.

I was the opposite of Taylor. I would sit in class, pondering how anyone could comprehend electrons whizzing round radio circuits, with their condensers charging and discharging millions of times a second, and the valve at the middle of it all miraculously straightening the whole shambles out so that you could hear the signal. It just didn't seem possible.

I did not find the commanding IQ which had got me into this mess of the slightest assistance. The only thing to do was something that I have always relied on when dealing with subjects that are beyond me. Without any real grasp, I just committed them lock, stock and barrel to the capacious memory that I had fortunately inherited from my father. So it was that I duly passed out of Yatesbury nowhere near the bottom of my class, but, secretly, a whited sepulchre of a radar expert.

We had nevertheless learned some useful techniques. One was the Drop Test. This was used, for example, when an infinitely expensive piece of gear such as the H2S, which gave you a flawless map of the ground beneath you from 30,000 feet, mysteriously refused to work. Then you just dropped it from a height of, say, six inches. The sharp impact shook up bad connections or bedded in slightly loose valves, and it nearly always worked. When it didn't, then you were in trouble.

An equally non-specific technique was the Screwdriver Test. When a piece of equipment such as the Gee navigational aid had packed up, then you turned your back on it and plunged the long blade of a well-insulated screwdriver into its refractory entrails. Either there was a flash and a bang, and you could write the set off, or it mysteriously mended its ways and began to function perfectly again.

There were some electronic terms of great poignancy which we acquired. For example, a curious form of connection was called a 'trombone mismatch', and when the carbon rings began to rattle in the rectifiers, this was known as 'chattering piles'.

We all knew that we were going to miss the permanent university-rag atmosphere of Yatesbury, and we did. Just before passing out, and hoisting the sparking red hand symbol of our trade on our left sleeves, we had a wonderful riot, during which the understanding NCOs in charge of us all turned the other way.

I had procured a large amount of a now-forgotten commodity, photographer's flash powder, and with this had been able to revert to a former hobby and make some very effective bombs. The fuse was provided by two matches, taped to the paper cylinder that held the charge. You struck them, and then had the few microseconds that it took to burn through the paper to get rid of the thing.

With these distributed among the members of the hut, we made a raid on our adversaries next door, with the result that the course after us very nearly only had a blackened shell to house them. The main reason that the fire went out was that someone else had produced equally large numbers of water bombs, and these extinguished the flash powder before it could do any real damage.

But I learned about much more than electronics at Yatesbury. For example, across my bedspace lived a Scotsman from Fowl's Heugh, who in civilian life was a Post Office engineer. He introduced me to the mysteries of receiver rest tapping in coin boxes, by which means you could bypass both the operator and the grasping little money box, and get right through to your correspondent free of charge. This knowledge seemed to spread rapidly, so that the camp's solitary red phone box was always full of airmen with their fingers vibrating in a blur on the receiver rest.

He also showed me a more sophisticated technique, involving a small square of rubber. To demonstrate the power of this, he called up his girl friend in Fowl's Heugh, and spoke cheerily to her for ten minutes without clattering a penny into the coin box.

In case modern technology has not eliminated this sly fraud, and as an erstwhile shareholder in British Telecom, I feel I should not ruin things for my former co-parceners by revealing how it was done. Suffice to say that it was a jolly welcome standby for an impecunious airman.

I also saw at first hand how a real entrepreneur set up the foundation of a business. An airman known to us all as Schwinkelbaum – now, not surprisingly, one of the mainstays of Madison Avenue – began canvassing round the huts for orders for personalised writing paper. He got quite a few takers, somehow printed up Basildon Bond himself to a professional standard, and delivered it to his customers for cash on the nail. Before we left the camp, he had a thriving stationery business among the thousands of airmen up on the windswept down beside the A4.

When the lorries took us away from Yatesbury to the nearest station, it was like leaving a much-loved school. There was a spirit there which I have rarely encountered since, and it seems a pity that modern young men and girls have little opportunity to enjoy the purposeful, disciplined hilarity of this kind of community.

By now, my father had opted to move from Cambridge, and taken up a zoological post in the Edward Grey Institute in Oxford. It was located in the School of Botany, opposite Magdalen.

The RAF had asked me where I would like to be posted next, and, perhaps unadventurously, I had suggested the airfield at Benson, where the Queen's Flight is now stationed. It was just three miles from the ancient, tumbledown cottage that my parents had bought in the quaint village of Berrick Salome.

I duly arrived there in the middle of the night having walked across the moonlit fields carrying my kitbag and the rest of my military gear from the village of Benson two miles away, where the bus dropped me. It was the first time that I had been home since they moved into The Yews, and I was struck by the suitability of the place for the two of them. The newer part at the front was built in 1615, and had been at different times a smithy, a Post Office and a village shop.

Subsequently, the house had fallen into the hands of one 'Stepper' Dance, who lived there for quite a few years. He was a large-scale DIY man, of the ramshackle variety, so that quite a lot of his work – notably the bathroom, perched half over the garden at eave level at the back of the structure – looked as if it might detach itself and fall into the raspberry canes one day.

In order to make The Yews available for sale, 'Stepper' had moved conveniently into a large chicken hut in a remote part of the garden, which he reserved to himself when he signed the contract for the rest. There, he and the delightful Mrs Dance lived for several years, providing help and comfort to my father as parts of the former Dance mansion fell down. This sounds like hyperbole, but in fact, the ancient clunch wall of my father's study, together with the wall of the room above, shortly began to keel slowly into the garden, so that shafts of sunlight came in through the widening crack.

This may have been because the water table was only three feet under the floor, which made it possible to have a shallow well just outside the window of my father's workroom. Consequently, the ground on which the house stood was permanently soaked, and had difficulty in supporting the weight of all Stepper's additions.

Initially, the huge tank in the roof, balanced precariously, in true Dance fashion, on a couple of shaky beams just above what was to be my bed, had to be filled daily by five hundred strokes of a hand pump in the kitchen. But eventually we electrified this, just before the local analyst condemned the water on the grounds that it was a soup of intestinal debris that ran into the water table from the cowsheds next door.

It was not only the safari-like adventure that made my parents love their strange little house. The near-acre of garden was of great fertility, and rapidly filled up with an inexhaustible series of foreign plants that they collected from the numerous countries that they visited.

Flowers were particularly welcome if they had a colourful history. A geum from the Temple of Jupiter in the Peloponnesus rioted everywhere, a *Scilla Hemispherica* that I bagged from the topmost point of Spyglass Hill in Gibraltar was proudly pointed out, as was a large peach tree grown from a stone sucked clean in Treviso. A house leek on the rockery which I had found on the Franz Joseph glacier was supposed to occur only in Spain, and my father speculated that it must have fallen out of the boot turnup of a galloping Habsburg messenger on his way to Vienna.

The rhubarb only came from a few miles up-river at Dorchester-on-Thames, but it became notable by achieving proportions normally only seen in science fiction. This was claimed to be due to the power of pig stools, with which it was constantly anointed.

While I was on leave, I added to Stepper's gimcrack creations by doing some electrical work, drawing on my recent arduous training at Yatesbury. The resulting lights worked, at least for a time, but their wiring would have given the Electricity Board the vapours if they had seen it.

In fact, my parents moved into Berrick Salome just in time to catch a number of octogenarians with personal memories of the 1860s. My father was so taken by the stories that they had to tell – working in the fields seven days a week, and walking a round trip of twenty miles to do so – that he later published a book called *The Departed Village* through Oxford University press. Illustrated by David Gentleman, it is a striking picture of how different our lives were only a century ago.

Crouched in a hollow under the friendly cover of one of the last spurs of the Chiltern Hills, Berrick was a village that time had forgotten. Houses four and five hundred years old abounded, and the church, which looked as if a few of the twiddly bits might have been added by Stepper, had a Saxon font.

Berrick boasted a renowned poacher called Wizzy Green, and to this day anyone who goes to the pub called the Home Sweet Home at the south end of the village will see his twelve bore hanging on the wall above a brass plate saying simply 'Wizzy's Cannon'.

There was also a middle-aged woman living in some state at the far end whom village gossip always referred to as 'The Strumpet', claiming that her natural haunt was the codpiece of any drunken farm labourer. This was the kind of poisoned speculation that adds to village life.

I spent a week or so of leave at The Yews, following my father round fields while he re-discovered the quail in Britain. He did this with the aid of bird whistles imported from hunting shops in the several European countries where these pretty little things are shot by the score for the table. Apparently unknown to Oxfordshire ornithologists, there were quails skulking in most of the county's cornfields, who responded with a musical peeping to my father's simulated cries. He was so enthused by this sound that he next bought a clock that produced the whistling of a quail instead of the traditional cuckoo.

I reported to my new camp at Benson. Its presence was already very obvious at home because our house was almost in line with the main runway, and Spitfires and Mosquitoes, in the honourable light blue livery of the photographic squadrons, screamed over the house in droves every flyable day.

We moved temporarily into more huts, then were bussed over to Chalgrove airfield a few miles away. It was now winter again, and the freezing nights we spent in Nissen huts on this abandoned airfield were a re-run of the refrigerated nights we spent at Thetford. Finally, the sergeant who came to fetch us every morning took pity on his icy, chilblained charges, and had us moved to that rare phenomenon, the pre-war brick barrack blocks on the station itself. Although these looked nice, and were comfortably heated, I nearly got electrocuted in there one evening. I was having a shower in the basement bath area, when I was felled to the porcelain footwell by a substantial electric shock.

Wriggling out of the live water, I staggered upstairs to my bedspace, thinking that I would report this hazard when I got my breath back. But, before I could do so, there came a terrible scream from downstairs. I ran down with others, and we found another airman going blue at the extremity, who had received an even more powerful shock. He was revived with the traditional therapy for those laid out by electricity. A bit later, it was found that another airman had earthed his defective radio to a water pipe by his bed, and in fact, the water system was live with 220 volts.

I began my work as a professional. The radar workshop was in the base of the control tower, so that we had a panoramic view of the gorgeous hardware flown by 82 Squadron, which I had been posted to.

Apart from the sleek Spitfires, mostly Mark XIXs, and the Mosquitoes, specially lightened so that they would do nearly 500 m.p.h. in a straight line when getting home with their valuable pictures, we also owned a couple of Lancaster bombers, one of which had just come back from doing an aerial survey covering most of East Africa. The beautiful Spitfires had no radar gear in them, only simple radios, so that there was no excuse for us to work on them, but the Mosquitoes were packed with electronics, from radar altimeters to Rebecca, a device to get them back safely into fogbound airfields. And the Lancs had even more, including the 120-valve H2S, and the American

Loran receivers. It was rather a responsibility, working on a sensitive piece of gear that some aircrew's life might depend on in bad weather, and it took me some time to get the confidence to attack it with vigour, and not just tiptoe round its silently inactive corpse waiting for an NCO to come and hold my hand.

Although it was by now more than a year after the end of the war, there were still heroic figures heaped with medals taking the aircraft up daily. And there were plenty of stories of terrible crashes that had happened to squadron contemporaries.

Because the reconnaissance aircraft flew so high, there were severe problems for the pilot if any interruptions to his oxygen supply took place at 35,000 feet. One Squadron Leader had landed on a German nightfighter base at Geelen in Holland when semi-conscious from an oxygen failure. He realized at the last minute that he was presenting an eager German unit with a Spitfire, and took the only course he could of retracting the undercarriage as he skimmed down the hostile runway so that the plane was effectively wrecked. And another pilot, a warrant officer, had wandered round the night sky barely conscious before crashing into the Chiltern Hills.

I had not been at Benson very long when another posting came through. This was to 544 Squadron at Aldergrove in Northern Ireland. Nowadays, the knowledge that a 19-year-old was being posted to this world capital of bigotry would have sent a shudder though his family, but when I arrived there, the only indications of the troubles to come were the liberal daubing of *Sod the Pope* on downtown walls, and the fact that, when I went to a Belfast dance shortly after my arrival, the first girl I asked to shuffle round with me said solemnly 'Are ye a Protestant or a Catholic?' before she would agree to my putting my arms round her.

The main purpose of the Squadron's presence in Northern Ireland was that they flew their ageing Handley Page Halifax bombers over a thousand miles into the middle of the Atlantic every morning at 4 a.m. in order to get weather information on which to base the Services' weather forecast. The codename of this hazardous exercise was *Bismuth*.

The fact that it was dangerous was illustrated when one aircraft disappeared so completely that the only trace found was

134

one big wheel floating in Lough Neagh. And another Halifax had a propeller fly off over the Atlantic and come whirring into the fuselage just in front of the pilot.

The groundcrew used to parade round the aircraft in the grey light of dawn, waiting to remedy any defects that might manifest themselves during the run up. As the huge Hercules rotary engines were accelerated to their peak RPM, the banks of air-cooled cylinders inside their cowlings glowed cherry red in the dimness.

Because large seabirds were a hazard to aviation at Aldergrove, a Corporal Falconer was stationed there to chase them away, and sometimes an officer from flying control would whizz round the perimeter track in his Hillman pick-up, firing Very lights to frighten any flocks of plovers that settled too near the duty runway.

Just as at Thetford, one side of Service life at Aldergrove was highly regimented, and the other half was like a grown-up playschool. The barrack blocks were rigorously inspected for perfect alignment of the folded bedding every morning, and our faces were carefully studied for runaway stubble. But I could drive to the public danger all over the airfield the three ton truck given me for my work, and nobody ever said a word. And we could beg flights on Dakotas going over to Silloth and Abingdon under the thin excuse of flight-testing our repairs, and we were positively encouraged to do so.

The radar section was regarded as a collection of eccentric eggheads, so that some of us made efforts not to disappoint our public. We tended to have Wurzel Gummidge haircuts straggling out from under our forage caps, and sometimes we turned up for the *Bismuth* dispatch in red polo-necked sweaters, or with pyjamas peeking out from under our battledresses.

It is hard to imagine now, but at weekends we used to go peacefully unarmed south of the border at Newry, through what is now bandit country, to the ration-free Irish Republic. The IRA had seemingly gone into a state of suspended animation at that time, but the inhabitants of Eire had a hearty dislike for us, so we did our best to conceal our identity.

One airman told me that he had reached a late stage in a cubicle in a public lavatory in Dundalk, when he realized that there was no toilet paper in it. Next door, he could hear a busy rustling, but on the wall he had already noticed a crude drawing of men streaming off a bus, with the legend 'starving bastards from the Six Counties coming south to eat all our food'.

'D'ye hov a bit of paper spare fer me, Paddy?' he called through the partition with the strongest Dublin accent he could muster.

'You can bloody well use your fingers, you dirty Irish sod,' said the unmistakable voice of one of his RAF comrades from the other side of the partition.

19

When a posting suddenly came through for me to go to Gibraltar, where another part of our squadron was stationed, I didn't quite have the moral fibre to refuse all my jabs, and tamely submitted. This is the reason that, forty years later, I still have a painful lump of yellow fever and assorted foreign bodies in my left deltoid.

We were sent on embarkation leave. I had by now acquired a beautiful girl friend, who lived in Hampstead. She was not only good to look at, she was also slightly crackers. I asked her what she would like to do on my last night in civilization, before gallantly going off to defend the Empire at the Pillars of Hercules.

She thought only for a very short period, then said that there were two things, really. One was to break into London Zoo at night, and the other was to lie on top of a high and close-knit privet hedge outside an unsuspecting house in Fairfax Avenue. Somehow, we duly got over the high fence which protected the animals' cages from people like us, and wandered in the darkness among the sinister growls and panting noises of the awakened animals. Finally, there were the sounds of running feet accompanied by shouts of alarm, and a flickering torch headed in our direction. Se we swiftly beat it back to the surmountable bit of fence by which we had entered. I was very anxious not to be caught because my father was a pillar of the Society at the time.

My implacable girl friend then insisted that I further prove my manhood on top of the privet hedge. We scrambled up to a height about seven feet above the pavement, both shrieking with laughter. Suddenly a window in the house opened, and a woman in curlers called us hooligans, and said she was phoning the police. I got hurriedly down, and only then realized that I was black from head to foot with the soot that abounded in vegetation in the Dark Ages before London became a smokeless zone.

By now, with all the excitement, I had missed the last Tube, so was obliged to walk the eight or so miles back to Kennington, where I was staying with the Vicar. Blacked up like a latterday Al Jolson, I duly roused him out of bed as dawn broke, and was never asked to stay in the Vicarage again.

RAF socks were made of very inferior wool in those days, and after a walk of such a distance, they always developed holes in the heels and often in the toes as well. A thoughtful Service provided us with a comprehensive 'housewife mending set', and I remember that the following day, riding on the Tube towards the West so that I could try for a lift out to my parents' house near Oxford, I sat with my socks off, assiduously inserting a large darn in each heel. This activity cleared a circle round me among my fellow passengers.

In those days, I was also interested in knitting, and was slowly putting together a six foot scarf. And this I also tended to pull out to work on when riding on public transport. Unfortunately, my sister had failed to give me instructions on how to cast off when it was finished, so I went hugely over-length, and never did decide how to end it.

The troopship was to go from Liverpool docks, and, by an extraordinary coincidence, I got a lift in a Vauxhall car only a mile or two from my parents' house which was going all the way to the place I wanted. The driver was an ex-Sergeant in the Royal Engineers who had been rescued from the beaches at Dunkirk, and he told me what he regarded as the true story of the shambles that preceded the miracle.

Apparently, as the troops made their way back through Northern France, many of the village women had been for weeks on their own without their husbands, and the beaten khaki-clad tide that flowed through the villages seemed like sexual manna to these frustrated ladies. According to him, most of his comrades barely had the strength to put their socks on in the morning, let alone to actually fight a rearguard action.

Once at Liverpool, we were given our laughably long khaki shorts, knee socks and safari shirts, and a series of lectures on the complex venereal diseases that awaited us just north of the

African continent. Then off we sailed on the elderly *Empire Hallidale* troopship.

My squadron was quartered some distance below the water-line. At night, after we had suspended our hammocks from hooks on the sides of the hull, we all swayed in unison to and fro, to the accompaniment in the steamy darkness of sounds of hopeless retching from men who had never been out of their native shires. We were all aware that in 1948 the high seas were still swilling with the many unexploded mines that had broken loose during five years of war, and that our chances of survival at that depth in the green tide would have been nil if one had brushed against our iron sides.

It made me glad that I was not making the trip a mere two years before, when we might have been stalked by wolf packs of German submarines as well.

We pitched our way through the Bay of Biscay, so familiar to me from my childhood, and watched the rusty Portuguese sardine boats tossing about as they towed their nets. Over the tannoy, endlessly, came the hits of the year, notably 'Peg of my Heart'.

I do not know how many men there were on the boat, but it must have been thousands. We ate our very basic food in endless relays, and the lavatories were only just able to cope with the blue and khaki-clad hordes. Sometimes you had to wait hours to have a shave, and many of us took to scraping away at our faces in remote corners of the deck.

I had not been to Gibraltar for fourteen years, and it was a great relief after a week of total loss of privacy to see from miles away in the Atlantic its stranded-whale silhouette gleaming whitely. In those days, there were still the brown hulks of five freighters half-submerged in the anchorage outside the harbour. They had been sunk by human torpedoes, mainly Italian, who had slid across the few miles of sea separating Gib from the neutral Spanish town of Algeciras.

We quickly settled into our new huts in the North Front camp, built right up against the wire of the Spanish frontier. The runway had recently been extended, and ran across the road from Spain which passed beside the camp. It had been the scene of some terrible crashes, notably the one that lost us

General Sikorski, and, shortly after I arrived, a four-engined Halifax had a bit of brake trouble while landing, and smashed into the control tower before bursting into flames. It was a fine pyrotechnic display, but fortunately no one was hurt.

Motivated by my genetic urge to examine my habitat from every angle, I spent my first free day walking right round the Rock, examining the great water catchment areas on the east side. These caught the frequent drip that descended from the plume of cloud above that streamed out over the Mediterranean. This was caused by the damp Atlantic air being cooled by three degrees as it went up 1200 feet to get over the bulk of the limestone crag.

I climbed Spyglass Hill as well, and collected the *Scilla Hemispherica* that I mentioned earlier for my mother. On the way down the exhausting line of steps from the top, I passed the famous colony of Barbary apes on whose survival the future of the Rock is thought to depend. Probably one of the young females that was gibbering at me as I passed within a couple of feet was on heat, because seconds later I heard a terrible scream, and saw Jack, the pack leader, racing down the steps after me, yellow fangs bared. He looked about the size of a large Labrador, and I could see that I would not last long in a fight with him. I turned tail and leaped down the stonework, three steps at a time. But he was still gaining on me. One of the soldier keepers saved me with a shout from below.

'Don't run,' he bawled, 'turn and swear at him.'

It took an effort of will to arrest my flight, but I did so, and he was barely two yards away when I exploded in obscenities in my best throaty sergeant's roar. With surprising agility, he came to a halt in one stride, chattered spittle at me, then turned and fled. I recognized that I had made a mistake that my father never made – encouraging an animal to attack by being cowardly.

Our huts were the omnipresent RAF issue, but the washing arrangements certainly weren't. A large tank stood between each duo of huts, full of seawater pumped out of the bay, and we were issued with a special soap that could still produce a bit of a lather even in brine. The first few times that you bathed in it, it left behind a sticky sensation as the salt crystals dried out on your skin.

My companions in the hut were the usual strange mixture. One was frighteningly ugly, and was always known as 'Brute'. Another, at nineteen, was already married. One day, one of the airman asked him what it was like to have a woman at his beck and call whenever he wanted.

'I knows what you mean,' he answered, grinning, 'Well, I tells yer, it's orl right as long as yer don't look at it. Puts yer orf yer breakfast if yer does.'

We mostly developed our own distractions quite quickly in this alien environment. I had always been a strong swimmer, and took to ploughing round the bay on the western side for hours on end. When I got tired, I would swim up to one of the sunken freighters and pull myself on board for a sunbathe. Jellyfish were one hazard, and I occasionally saw sawfish, but they never showed any interest in my puffing, crawling figure.

I also used to take the ferry across to Algeciras and walk in the hinterland over towards Cadiz. It was in those days a completely empty tract of country, although I doubt if it is now. I occasionally fell into step with leather-accoutred young Spanish soldiery, and had some strange conversations with them in my best Spanish. Spain was still going through the *Todo por la Patria* phase that bedevils all dictatorships – they think that constant shouting and daubing of patriotic slogans will hide the fact that they have insufficient to eat, and that the economy is a shambles. You can see the same symptoms in many countries more recently, notably Romania and Iran. But the young Spanish soldiers were very interested in England, and unanimously admired Churchill.

'*Es un hombre con dos cojones,*' (He is a two-testicled man), said one Spanish private, paying his highest compliment.

I also revived my interest in gun making. One of my fellow radar mechanics made a most successful weapon from my original design, with the stock constructed out of the wood of an old Spanish chest of drawers which we found on a tip.

It fired .22 cartridges as usual, and was devastingly accurate. One day, in a burst of high spirits, we shot to pieces the perspex and aluminium specimen kit lay-out that ornamented our hut.

141

Attracted by the crackle of unauthorized musketry, the sergeant on duty came hurrying round from the guardroom not far away. The new gun vanished into a sandwich of blankets, and someone hastily put his hat over the wreck of the kit layout. We all stood around in self-conscious innocence, while the sergeant sniffed the dense cloud of cordite in the hut.

'Wha's going' on in 'ere?' he said, in the manner of policemen everywhere.

'My cat let off a Spanish firework,' said our Geordie inmate. Everyone knew that he had a black and white kitten that slept down his bed.

'Wha's he bloody doin' wiv a firework? And 'ow the buggery did 'e let it orf?' snarled the sergeant.

'He was carrying it around and put it down in that ashtray with a lighted cigarette.'

The sergeant looked from one desperately serious face to the other, then said heavily, 'Any more of this buggerin' about and you'll all be doing jankers until you're demobbed.' He stamped off.

But I have to be honest and say that the main hobbies of my comrades-in-arms centred round the bordellos in Gibraltar Street, just over the border, and getting leglessly drunk.

There was a little hut just over our side of the border in which soldiery returning from romantic missions were supposed to carry out running repairs, which mainly consisted of dusting their pubes with anti-crab powder, and squirting a savage ointment in appropriate places. There were also posters all round the walls that would have cured the squeamish for ever from even holding hands with the opposite sex.

Thinking to do them a good turn, I had taught my hut comrades to say in Spanish to any ladies over the border who offered their services '*Quiero ver a su certificado medical de Usted.*' Spanish law at the time required street ladies to be registered, and to carry a form with their picture on, rather like the temporary version of a British passport. This had to be stamped every three days by a doctor who examined them at the same time. A small guarantee, but a useful one.

But only a month or two later, a Yorkshireman called Tom

staggered into my bedspace, showing a part which was distinctly the worse for wear.

''Ere, Einstein, what do you think is 'appenin' to me bloody John Thomas?' he queried.

'You've got a dose, that's what,' I answered, 'you didn't check some floozie's medical card.'

'It wasn't that, mate,' he said, 'I was too pissed to read it when she showed it to me. Couldn't get me bloody eyes to focus.'

He underwent a course of penicillin injections with large bore needles that was half punishment and half therapy. It rapidly cured him, but he crossed Gibraltar Street off his visiting list after that.

An unfortunate thing happened to me while I was working on a radar set in the tail of a Halifax. I thrust a test probe into the large, throbbing box without checking that the insulation was still in place. It wasn't, and I got a 5000-volt shock which flung me down the fuselage until I was stopped by the Elsan.

I did not feel quite so good about electricity for a bit, so that it was a relief when the smart new Education Officer marched into the radar section one day and told my boss that he had permission to misemploy me as deputy Education Officer. This was the cushy number that every Serviceman dreams of. I spent my days in the large, airy hut that housed the books, films and records with a tall, gawky Gibraltarian girl whom the camp called Big Mary.

Apart from holding record concerts which were attended by a surprising number of airmen, I began teaching French and German. It was my first contact with mature students, and I was most gratified to see that they listened attentively and tried to improve, unlike the schoolboys I had so recently left, who concentrated on lubricious thoughts, and flicking ink pellets round the class while Sir was writing on the board.

Some leave came up. One of my pupils was a daring Irishman who had recently taken a fortnight in Tangier and Morocco on his own, and I decided that sounded fun.

Having crossed the Straits in a De Havilland Rapide which took off sideways on our vast runway, I checked into one of Tangier's major hotels. I had only been in my room a few minutes, when the smooth-looking proprietor called Bendahan came in. He understood that I was a friend of Paddy Coyne's from Gibraltar, and all friends of Paddy's were friends of his. Would I like to come to the circus with him that night?

Slightly uncertain of his intentions, but used by now to strange invitations, I thanked him and agreed. It was a remarkable evening. He owned an Armstrong Siddeley Hurricane, and it was a matter of honour for him to drive it flat out through the narrow and encumbered streets round the Souk. I saw a tide of Arabs parting like the Red Sea as this Jehu bore down on them, missing dismembering them by inches all along the route. He had obviously been doing it for years and somehow escaped manslaughter, so I settled down to find it exhilarating.

We took our seats at the circus, which was on the beach on the east side. The performance was full of good things; my favourite was a bullskin occupied by two athletic men, who pursued various clowns round the ring, finally knocking them down and passing gallons of water over their recumbent forms. While I was throwing myself about in hilarity at this, I suddenly heard a commotion on my right side. I was next to a pretty Arab girl, and it appeared that I had accidentally touched her. Her boy friend had jumped to his feet, eyes flashing, and announced to the world that he was going to knife me. So saying, he pulled a curved blade out of his trouser pocket, and adopted an on guard stance.

Bendahan, who had the advantage over me that he understood what the young man was ululating, brushed the blade aside with great sang froid, explained that I was an Englishman, and therefore bound to be rather more careless with my extremities than a Son of the Prophet, and we all subsided back into our seats to watch more clowning.

After the circus, we went to a night club which, I discovered later, was also owned by Bendahan. Belly dancers appeared one after the other, oscillating their abdomens. Bendahan had asked me what I preferred to drink, and for some reason I had said iced Benedictine. I did not notice at first that my glass was being continually refilled.

Presently, he turned to me and asked if I played any

instrument. I answered thickly that I could manage the piano a bit, without adding that I would probably be much better at it if the leather-jockstrap-wearing Piggy Reynolds had left me alone to practise.

'It's all yours,' he said, waving me to the huge white grand that stood centre stage. I got groggily to my feet, and staggered up the steps on to the stage. Bendahan made some announcement in Arabic which I could not understand. I sat down at the blurred ivories. At that moment, I could remember the fingerwork for only two ditties. One was Chopin's *Polonaise in A*, which I had been painfully deciphering from the music on a NAAFI piano with a couple of notes missing, and the other was *Jesu, Joy of Man's Desiring*, which I had picked out on the harmonium years before. I sat down and began to play the latter, resisting the temptation to accompany myself with the anthem in a thin tenor.

My fingers were moving rather stiffly, but the Benedictine was certainly helping my stage fright, and I used lots of loud pedal. I am not sure how many verses I gave the assembly, but it was probably more than Dame Myra Hess usually played. Finally, I ended with a crashing and not very harmonious chord, and applause filled the room.

We had been joined by the hotel manager by the time I got back to my seat. He was a rather ingratiating young Spaniard only a few years older than me. We all left together and repaired to Bendahan's flat. I was becoming rather uneasy, and when the young manager showed signs of leaving the room, I asked rather truculently where he was going.

'I have to search Mr Bendahan's flat for assassins. It is part of my duties,' he said shortly.

'I'll come round with you, then,' I said. We spent the next twenty minutes rummaging through the vast, richly furnished building, looking behind Louise XV armoires, and under richly tasselled beds. The Benedictine heightened the sense of unreality. When we got back to where Bendahan sat, now looking like a frog, the manager reported that all was clear.

'I am going home,' I said resolutely, 'shall I get a taxi?' It was already about 3 a.m. Rather grudgingly, Bendahan took me on another wild ride through the now mercifully deserted streets in his Hurricane. But his hospitality had not quite finished. I was just getting exhaustedly into bed when there was a soft knock on the door. I opened it, and a willowy girl stood there, dressed like something escaped from a harem.

'What do you want?' I asked, rather nonplussed.

'Mr Bendahan say perhaps you like some jeegajeeg now,' she replied huskily.

20

In the morning, I set off by train at 6 a.m. for Casablanca. Sitting grimly upright on my slatted wooden Third Class seat, I watched the early morning sun rising as we pulled slowly out of Tangier. The fine sandy beach seemed to be dotted with heaps of manure, like a well-fertilized autumn meadow in England. As I watched, one after another the heaps rose majestically in the gathering daylight. They proved to be Arabs who had spent the night sleeping cosily wrapped in their robes.

When I look back, I must have been strangely clad for this sub-tropical journey; I was wearing brown English corduroys and a green Harris tweed sports jacket which had been made for me in Gibraltar by the Government's tailor, a Mr Brown. It had a poacher's pocket on the left hand side into which I could fit most of my luggage – my father had always told me what a practical feature this was.

I think I must have thought that I looked a bit of a dog in this outfit, because I stuck to it grimly in temperatures which in the desert went up to 120 degrees Fahrenheit.

Casablanca proved to be a town of nearly a million inhabitants, sprawling whitely round the bay. Although the French had occupied it only since 1907, their presence had thoroughly permeated the hotels and restaurants, and sometimes it seemed more like France than Morocco. Very Moroccan, however, were the beggars, who followed me everywhere, usually either trying to sell cigarettes, for which I had no use, or the services of their sisters.

Thinking that I ought to explore the culture as well as the countryside thoroughly, I went to an Arab concert, where a lot of wailing through the nose in semitones went on, accompanied by the frenzied clashing of strange instruments. Finally, I cut my losses and slunk out to a cafe nearby. A young man sitting at the next table with a beautiful girl noticed me staring gloomily into my beer, and asked in French where I came from. I told him. In those days, Anglophiles were more common than they have been since we engaged a rabble of football hooligans as our social ambassadors.

Alberto and his sister proved to be great admirers of England, and took to me with enthusiasm as an escaped specimen. They even escorted me over the desert in another train to the ancient red-walled provincial capital of Rabat. Alberto wanted to take me for a visit to one of its famed bordellos, but when we got there, a Spahi two metres high stood guard in flowing robes outside, barring our way with a big drawn sword. Alberto asked him what the matter was, and was told that it was the Spahis' night in there, and no one else could enter. From inside the building came screams and sounds of smashing glass to back up what he said.

Finally, feeling quite disoriented by my carefree weeks in Africa, I put on my uniform again in Gibraltar, and went back to work with Big Mary.

Sitting in my haven of an Education Section, listening more often than not to Stan Kenton's 'Peanut Vendor', and a hopelessly indigestible language record on Arabic, I debated with myself what I should do next in life.

Occasionally the wild thought of signing on in the RAF occurred, but it rapidly vanished again because I had been branded as having the wrong IQ to fly. Perhaps I should try medicine again when I got out and went up to the university? But there would be all that awful physics and chemistry to grind through before I actually saw a patient. Perhaps the Law? But then one would be obliged to defend people whom one knew to be guilty as well as despicable, and one might just be so successful that they would be released to do it again.

My father wrote me a letter making two suggestions for future careers. One was the police, and the other, the Diplomatic Corps. I smiled wanly at the thought of either of them.

The day dawned for embarkation on another troopship and the voyage back to England. I was really sorry to leave the implacably sunny climate, my dogged voyages round the blue-green waters of the bay, the hotch-potch of nationalities that made up the 28,000 inhabitants, and the feeling of being at the crossroads between Europe and Africa, with the ability to go into either in twenty minutes.

But I felt that I had not wasted my time there. My Spanish was now highly colloquial, my Gibraltar-issued passport ensured me interesting journeys all over the world later because I needed a visa for every country on earth, and the NAAFI piano had greatly strengthened my Chopin Polonaise.

My homecoming into the drizzle-blanketed Liverpool dock was made all the less agreeable by the fact that a stern-faced Customs man chose me to do a meticulous searching job on. He even squinted angrily at the cotton reels and needles in my 'housewife'. A senior officer came up and said that I wasn't to take it personally; it was just that they made a habit of picking on one person out of each group just as a warning to the others. I derived some satisfaction from the fact that the fountain pen in my breast pocket concealed under its shiny cap the barrel of the latest weapon that I was finishing.

We went to Lytham St Annes to be demobilized. I remember walking into the uneventful little centre for an evening in a mournful pub, where somehow I picked up a woman some years older than me who worked during the day as a Civil Servant. To my surprise, she said she would walk some of the three miles back to camp with me – Lancashire girls at that time were mostly pretty battle-weary where airmen were concerned.

Passing a small public park in the darkness, she suddenly dragged me in, and began to embrace me with breathy passion. For a moment, I thought my luck was in, then my wandering hands identified an armoured corset protecting her with as much efficacy as a Cromwellian soldier's justaucorps. Then I also realized that her passionate kisses were pushing a double set of false gnashers quite a long way down her throat. I decided to extricate myself with all the speed that I could without unduly hurting her feelings.

The following day, we were issued with our demob clothes. Because of my strange shape – a Moss Brothers assistant years later described it as 'Colonial' – I could not get my chest into the suits, until the soldier doing the fitting had a brainwave and reached me down a fine tweed marked 'Portly'. This fitted perfectly round the shoulders, but had room for another chap inside the waistband. Eventually, the trousers were taken in eight inches, and all was well.

My parents had decided to take me on holiday to Northern Ireland immediately I got back. Nowadays, that might sound a quite absurd thing to do, but in that happy time before part of the population of that blessed Province went mad, we spent happy days roaming the glens of Antrim, marching about on the Giant's Causeway, and, needless to say, rowing about in the bay.

I was suffering a certain amount of cultural shock; when one has been for two years in the company day and night of blokes whose every second word is an oath, and whose lurid turns of phrase revolve mainly around sex, drink and military matters, it is quite hard to adjust to the gentle warmth of family life.

I also discovered that rather a change had taken place in the attitude of young women to me. Now that I had a raffish ex-Service air about me, as well as a North African tan and hair burnt blond, I found to my surprise that girls were asking me to dance rather than the reverse, and not questioning me about my religion before taking the floor, either.

One morning, I had only been in bed for twenty minutes in our hotel when my mother came to wake me with a cup of tea that I was almost too exhausted to drink after an unplanned night in a barn. And the daughter of the hotelier took to slipping into my room at night and stripping off my bedclothes to provoke me. Even the most unattractive of us can have a brief Golden Age, and I guess that, at least romantically, my few weeks in Ireland as a twenty-year-old was that time.

But most normal young men and women suddenly realize that they have outgrown the nest, and that realization came to me in Antrim. In fact, I never stayed more than a few days at a time at home after that, and even then I was raring to get back with my contemporaries as soon as possible, just as my own son does now.

Life had one agreeable surprise for me. I had taken the Cambridge Entrance Exam before I left school two years before. It was in a huge room in the Market Hall, and I was aware that I had not done terribly well. Shortly before I came up for the ordeal, I had read somewhere of a wretched fellow whose performance in an exam had been pathetic because he was haunted by the couplet:

Then it's punch, punch, punch with care.
Punch in the presence of the passenger.

For some absurd reason, I conjured up this rhyme early in the first paper, and it dinned in my head as I tried to work. I subsequently heard nothing from the group of colleges for which I had applied, so assumed the worst.

Then, when I came out of the RAF, I wrote to the excellent Professor Thorpe, who by then was Senior Tutor of Jesus College, to know what form of entreaty might succeed with his College. To my great surprise, he replied that they had held a confirmed place for me ever since what I had believed to be the débâcle in the Market Hall.

So up to Cambridge I rapidly went. The colleges were full of what was known as 'returned warriors'. Some of them had been colonels, wing-commanders, and even captained quite large warships in the recent conflict. They certainly suffered a much more serious cultural shock even than I did when they had to be into College by 10.30 p.m. every night, and were not allowed to shut the doors of their rooms – 'sporting your oak' it was called in dialect – if they had a lady of any age in there.

The warlike tendencies of that era of undergraduates were underlined on 5 November 1948, the second month after I came up. A serious riot took place in the town centre. An ex-Commando officer let off a charge of gun-cotton on the lawn in front of the Senate House, and broke seventy panes of priceless hand-made glass.

I watched an athletic undergraduate shinning up the nine lampposts on Market Hill one by one, and kicking out the light while hanging upside down. He has sat in the House of Lords for the last thirty years, and I often wonder if he remembers this exploit as he dreams debates away on the red leather benches there.

Another activity on that infamous night was the seizing of passing cars travelling up Trinity Street. They were brought to a halt by twenty or so men grabbing every projection. Then the rear end would be lifted off the ground, while the terrified driver usually revved the engine frantically in an effort to get away. Suddenly the back wheels, spinning madly, would be dropped back on the macadam, and the car would depart at speed in a random direction like a runaway rocket.

Another effort was the uprooting of a Belisha beacon from the pavement outside Marks and Spencer, and its subsequent crashing through the window of that establishment. The ranks of the returned warriors were a little thinner after this example of a civilian Mess Rag Day – seventy-five of them were sent down.

I was a bit slow to integrate myself into the society; for one thing, most of my contemporaries had been various sorts of officer, and my best efforts had not got me beyond local, honorary and temporary sergeant because of the violent contraction of the RAF that was taking place. It seems odd now, but when one has been accustomed for two years to treat the officer class as demi-gods, it needs a bit of re-adjustment to recognize that they were just the sort of people that I had been brought up with.

My 21st birthday came upon me three days after I had gone up, and I well remember buying myself a drink in solitary state in a pub called the Bath in Benet Street. After a bit, I was joined by a rather ingratiating Northern aristocrat and his two toadies. He was subsequently to achieve an unwanted notoriety by mowing down and killing three bedmakers in Trumpington Street.

I had already equipped myself with a suitably rakish bicycle, with a frame designed for a large child, so that the saddle always had to be ultimately extended. It only had one brake, the front one, which required tentative application. I had bought this trusty steed from the horse butcher in Benson, a colourful character by the name of Passy. The bicycle lasted throughout my three years, and, because of its rebarbative aspect, was never stolen.

Another undergraduate solved the theft-proofing in a different way; he broke off one of the horns of his handlebars, then re-learned the riding technique. No one else could ride it more than a few yards, so it too was never stolen.

There was a tendency to adopt radical solutions like that. My landlady in Jesus Lane was prone to rush up the stairs from the basement on rainy days to check whether I had wiped my feet before entering her Valhalla. So I took to hopping up the path on one brogue in the bad weather, subsequently changing to the dry one once inside, and hopping on into my room. The effort was worth it when I could hear the furious little Scotswoman inspecting her hall floor on her knees, without finding the slightest trace of a damp footprint.

One of the sights of Jesus College in those days was an English and classical Latin scholar called Dr Freddie Brittain. He was reported to be the son of a jobbing gardener in Barnet, and certainly his pronounced London accent would fit. Moon-faced, with beautifully thick and well-groomed hair, he had invented a strange activity called 'Roosting'. This was devised from the fact that the Jesus College arms involve a number of gallinaceous cocks, after the founder, whose name was Alcock. Freddie had filled his rooms in College with every conceivable variety of cock, ancient and modern, and, once his passion was known, old students sent him any cocks that they could lay their hands on round the world.

I never really got into Roosting, but those who did reported that the sessions consisted mainly of elaborate jokes about cocks, *double entendres* and a certain amount of mockery perhaps of religious exercises, or possibly Masonic ones.

Freddie had a formidable intellect, and he was my tutor for a bit. I think he preferred the company of the young ladies from Girton and Newnham, who came to him for Latin. He usually referred to them as the 'Britannic Battery'.

He was perhaps the most notable card among the dons, but the others had their moments. One history tutor had an eighteenth-century wickerwork condom on his mantelshelf, with the coat of arms of a noble family on the business end, which was said to be made out of the *caecum* of a lamb. The Dean, Gardner-Smith, seemed already to be as old as Methuselah, but he nevertheless lasted another thirty years, and finally died widely mourned not far off his century.

But Dr Laurence Picken was the most fascinating of the lot. He had recently gained the Linnaean Medal for contributions to biochemistry, which was his principal subject. But he was also a formidable linguist, speaking several dialects of Chinese, as well as Turkish, Albanian, and all the other European tongues. And, finally, he was one of the best musicians in the university, coping equally well with the spinet, organ, Chinese funeral bagpipe and hundreds of other ethnic instruments. He proved beyond doubt the standard of his musicianship when he was later appointed Director of the School of Musicology at Madingley.

Years later, I was entertaining a Turk called Kemal Atabay, who owned a pharmaceutical company in his native land. With his fine-looking daughter as an interpreter, I took him up for a weekend visit to Cambridge. We called unannounced on Laurence Picken, who greeted Atabay in perfect Turkish, and lifted a rare Turkish instrument like a lute off his wall and began to play it. The Turk was ravished, and said that he had never heard this rare lute played so well outside a musical museum at home.

Laurence's inexhaustible omniscience often caused me pleasure. Once I asked him at the end of the summer term what he had planned for the succeeding three months.

'Well,' he answered thoughtfully, 'first of all I have to go to Skopje where I have been asked to give a lecture in Serbo-Croat on the bagpipe in Eastern Turkey. Then I am going on a collecting trip round Anatolia to obtain some more instruments.'

He had the habit of wearing an oversize pancake-shaped beret on some of these trips. Made of white felt, it came from Washington University, and had a silver roaring lion embroidered on it with the motto; '*Lux sit*'. On a particular trip to Bulgaria, one of Laurence's companions was the other British authority on the biochemistry of the cell. He had had a long-standing feud with Laurence, and indeed had reviewed the latter's book in the *TLS*, and commented acidly on that occasion that 'it is full of the quirks of greystones scholarship.' This hostile individual had followed Laurence down from the top of a Bulgarian mountain up which the visiting savants had been taken. For some time he looked down on his adversary in silence, then, overcome with academic rectitude, he leaned forward, tapped Laurence on the shoulder, and snapped, 'Not lux *sit*, Picken. *LUX EST.*'

21

By the time that I arrived in Cambridge, my best second language had become Spanish, because of all the chatting up that I had been able to do in Spanish Morocco and across the frontier beside my hut. Unfortunately, it was not one of the tongues that I had put my name down to study, so that I could see a crash course was necessary in French and German. In fact, Trevor Jones, my German tutor and the man who wrote the scholarly German dictionary for Harrap, regularly held his head in his hands with despair when I attempted to make jokes in the language he was trying to teach me.

Germany was still not accessible to civilians at the end of 1948, however, so I resolved that my first total immersion would be in France. With some excitement, I arrived at the Gare St Lazare on the first day of my Christmas holidays, and set off down the Ligne des Sceaux to the Cité Universitaire.

In those colourful days at the Cité, it was possible to meet apparently irresponsible students of one's own age who had spent three years from the age of fifteen onwards crouching in frosty foxholes on the Russian front. Or twenty-five-year-old ex-fighter pilots who had acquired their premature crows' feet peering month after month into the sun for the enemy. Such people had no fear of eccentricity or discomfort, and an eager competition developed between us to see who could live in the cheapest and most satirical way.

Not being as battle-hardened as some, I chose the line of least resistance, and tipped fifty old francs to the concierge in the *Ecole Agronomique* for him to hang a *Hors Service* notice outside a lavatory door on the second floor. Inside, safely locked in, there was just room to suspend a hammock diagonally between the water pipes. The notice was not an absolute guarantee of peace, however. There were some desperate inmates who would run down the corridor with their eyes, as the French say, not completely opposite the eyeholes. They would batter on the door in the early morning, shouting '*Nom d'un pipe!*' and '*Bourgre d'animal!*' as they sought entry for pressing personal reasons. And I had to be very careful about locking up when I went out, otherwise the site would be garlicky and uninhabitable when I got back.

A Mexican film student called Tiberio was my nearest neighbour. He lived in a broom cupboard which smelt wholesomely of polish and Eau de Javel. He had tried various ways of sleeping in there – lying on the single shelf in the foetal position, only inches below the ceiling, and suspended in a sort of Baby Bouncer from one of the broom hooks. Finally, he had settled for curling up on the grubby floor like a large dog.

Most of the students in the *Ecole Agronomique* lived in permanent semi-darkness anyway, because the clever young architect who had designed the place had put in huge sheets of glass on every outside wall. Apart from a few compulsive exhibitionists, for anything more intimate than changing your socks, exhausting yards of curtain had to be drawn, and the light put on. Most of my neighbours, who were often hospitable day and night in the French fashion, simply drew the curtains when they moved in, and lived their lives from then on in artificial light.

Of course, in my lavatory I never needed any such modesty screens. The same gifted architect had given me a window which opened into the lift shaft, so that a pleasant, oily-scented breeze came soughing in as the lift rose and sank like the plunger of a great pump. And unseen friends would shout cheering messages to me as they whizzed past in the cage.

The pipes round my domain had a savage symmetry. And sometimes they knocked magisterially, bringing down flecks of plaster. The remedy was a quick flush, to purge them of pressure.

To make the place a little more like home, I hung up a few press cuttings. One was about a nineteen-year-old English girl who had shown her patriotism by breaking a shop window on the Boulevard St Michel with her umbrella handle. She had done this because, prominently displayed inside, there had been a face of the British Queen superimposed on the body of a half-naked can-can dancer.

Another of my pictures showed the wrinkled features of an orang-utang called Babette, who had escaped from the Vincennes Zoo, and been recaptured in the Metro by a lorry driver who had offered her a cigarette which she had wolfed hungrily down, and waited expectantly for more.

It took us some time to discover all our fellow trogs. Sometimes we would go out visiting, tapping on the metal walls of little electric sub-stations, potting sheds, and half-collapsed air raid shelters, even, towards the end of the craze when things got rather exaggerated, down the inspection tunnels of sewers.

One of the kings of this student sub-culture was known as Toutac, short for Tout-Acne because of the Himalayan lumps on his face. He lived at the *Pavillon Britannique*, a place that most of us shunned because of its frenzied concierge. She did floor-to-ceiling checks of the place at unpredictable intervals, and seemed to have a personal radar which told her automatically if there were any illegal immigrants up among the twittering swifts in the voluminous roof space.

Toutac had turned up there one day in a workman's blue boiler suit, with a large tool box, saying that the *Service des Eaux* had decided that, in view of recent seismic disturbances, all water systems had to be inspected.

Once up among the towering neo-Jacobean roof timbers, he saw what he had hoped for: a cathedral-sized tank which must have held thousands of gallons. Out of his tool kit, he pulled a one-man rubber dinghy, blew into it until he felt faint, then moored it in the tank, hanging his worldly belongings on a handy angle of pipe.

He had taken care to anchor at the opposite end from the great ballcock and its gurgling entry pipe, and he claimed that the tides that rose and fell as lavatories flushed and baths ran in the building below were rather soothing. Toutac's single enduring problem was that of access. He solved it by organizing simple group activities among his many friends in the house. Before he ran in, he would put on oilskins, a sou'wester and a false red beard, so that he looked like an advertisement for cough lozenges. Then he would erupt through the door and race up the stairs, screaming 'Mayday, Mayday!'

As soon as he concierge saw him through her little inspection window, she would shout in turn *Merde, le barbu de nouveau.* and begin waddling up the stairs after him like something in an old American cartoon. Stolid British accomplices would rush out on to the landing to block her path, singing Rugby songs, while a mathematics student with the typically British name of Kropotkin would lift Toutac up through the trapdoor just outside his room. By the time that the concierge arrived, panting and fulminating, Toutac would have disappeared.

Then two things happened. First, Toutac fell out of his dinghy one night and nearly drowned in the freezing water. Then, even his friends began to complain of the rubbery taste of the tank water. The more unkind said that it was only a matter of time before bubonic acne raged through the building. In the face of growing public disapproval and the threat of having to confront the concierge alone, he sadly withdrew to the vegetable store under the student restaurant, where, in return for an occasional helping hand to the peeling man, he lived leguminously ever after.

One day, I was sitting in the cafeteria, eating between bouts of noisy hammering – you were expected to thump the table with the handle of your knife if anyone deviating from the norm in appearance came in. That day, a Scot in a ragged kilt had been hammered for minutes, as had a chap with a bloodstained bandage round his head after a road accident. In a moment of silence, I began boasting to the man opposite that I had been clever enough to incorporate a convenience into my student squat, thus solving one of the most awkward problems that people like Toutac had.

He listened impatiently for a minute or two, then said 'Me, I not only get free warmth and electricity. I also get a whole sewer to myself. Come, I show you.' We drank our coffee down to the iron filings from the ruined enamel urn, then walked out towards the *Pavillon de l'Indochine.* At an ordinary-looking point on the concrete road, he stopped, looked carefully round for the concierge military police, then whipped a bent door handle from his pocket and took up the manhole at his feet.

'*Entrez, je vous prie,*' he said politely. I clambered down the iron cleats on the wall. The heat from the great electric cables and the steam pipes verged on the sauna-like.

The place was lit with little neon lamps with crucifix shaped filaments, of the sort that burn steadily in French shrines since automation replaced the glowing oil lamp. They seemed to be powered by screwdrivers thrust boldly into the fat cables.

My guide took me on a crouching conducted tour past his bed, which was sprung with a roll of wire netting underneath an old hearthrug. Close by in the confined space was another trap door, mercifully tightly sealed, which led into the effluent pipe from the nearest *Pavillon*. A carboy of water for slaking his eternal tropical thirst, and a pile of books, completed the furniture.

'*Felicitations, mon vieux,*' I said, already beginning to get the vapours from the mixture of heat and claustrophobia.

Cash flow was an acute and chronic problem for all of us. One or two survived by selling their blood, half a litre at a time, to private clinics. They sometimes became prosperous, but were mostly too ghostly pale and breathless to enjoy it. Others sang in cracked voices in the gutters along the Boulevard St Michel, or cleaned windscreens at the traffic lights, fouling them all over again if the drivers did not tip them or became abusive.

And there was a lot of other entrepreneurial activity. One well-set-up lad would stand by the Mona Lisa hour by hour, waiting for the right sort of blue-rinsed tourist. Then, when one began gazing with synthetic rapture at the picture, he would tap her on the shoulder and say in his rumbling bass Charles Boyer voice, 'Madam, you are much more beautiful than this Mona.' The occasional lady would hit out with her travelling handbag full of smelling salts and diarrhoea remedies. This was just the kind of would-be Apache rapist that they had been warned against back home.

Most often, however, they would react with elephantine coyness, and end up buying the hungry fellow a meal in gratitude. Sometimes a whole string of meals, including breakfast. Once, a huge, hat-wearing husband emerged from behind the arras as Emile made his bid, and scored a bull with a punch designed to prevent his wife from being defiled. After that, Emile would follow a prospective quarry for a whole gallery before whipping out his compliment.

One of our favourite money-earning jokes was that developed by a tall, gaunt girl who for some reason called herself Arthenice, which was an anagram of her real name, Catherine. She would go to a different site each free afternoon, walking in step with an accomplice. They would always be tourist resorts, such as the Arc de Triomphe, the Panthéon, or Notre Dame.

When there were plenty of well-breeched-looking by-standers, she would fall in a heap on the pavement, going down like a rag doll, often showing her knickers or releasing one breast to increase consumer interest. Her accomplice would then make a short speech over her recumbent corpse: '*Rien à manger depuis trois jours – pauvreté écrasante – étudiante brillante*' etc. and, if they were lucky, a small collection would be made on the spot and they would both be driven home. There were limitations to this act – it required great fortitude to collapse in puddles in bad weather, and occasionally nosy old men would try to find the heartbeat, or want to undo the blouse further to free the breathing.

The phoney Jehovah's Witness squad was a failure. They set off round the Seventh Arrondissement, pushing their way into houses, rattling collecting boxes made out of cocoa tins, talking volubly about the hereafter, and picking their noses in order to make themselves so repulsive that everyone would want to pay to get rid of them as soon as possible.

Unfortunately, one of their early would-be victims proved to be a senior policeman, who unfurled his massive, oily revolver and demanded to see their credentials.

None of us felt the urge to do a real job, except some American fellow students, who became misty-eyed as they explained that they were following in the footsteps of many of their great men, who had seen themselves through High School, dirty-fingered from carrying newspapers or blacking boots. They tried to encourage us to follow this Protestant work ethic, but it never caught on. There was something so satisfying about going down to the culture-hungry queue at the Opéra, selling tickets printed on a student press, until a roar from the foyer indicated that the first one had been unsuccessfully presented. Then you legged it away to the Boulevard des Capucines, trying not to drop the wealth which you had just redistributed.

Some of us thought that there might be some steam in a latterday version of the Guy de Maupassant story about the sad, beautiful widow who lurked in graveyards preying on devastated males who came to mourn. One day a theology student who looked about fourteen in spite of his mature years decided to try.

Choosing a large, recently-erected granite mausoleum with a vitrified photo on it of a young woman who looked like Medusa, he stood sobbing with an arm across his eyes to hide their dryness, occasionally bleating *'Qu'est-ce que je peux bien faire sans ma chère Maman?'*

The first time that he tried it, he heard a passing black-clad figure remark loudly, *'Quel con,'* as he reached a bleating crescendo. But he must have improved his act later because a maiden lady took him up, and he moved into a life of such luxury that he was able to give up theology altogether.

The Mexican student film director Tiberio and I, after a few penniless weeks thrashing about trying to choose a racket that did not have too many criminal implications, teamed up with an English art student and trombonist called Jackson. He spoke no French, and we were therefore allowed to live modestly off his earnings, in return for a certain amount of marketing of his services.

He spent a solitary life in the warm boiler room under the Maison Cubaine – the Cubans were known in the Cité as *Les Canards*, because, as they said, *'Ils ont quand-même le cul bas.'*

After the day's lectures, the three of us would go round the *boîtes* of the Latin Quarter, getting permission for Jackson to blow it cool for short stands. Officially, I was his manager, and Tiberio was his secretary. When Tiberio went ostentatiously to the front with his collecting plate, I used to stand in the shadows by the door, grabbing any dodgers who tried to run out. When we were offered drinks, we always opted for milk, so that we got the extra protein; you could hardly ask for a sandwich.

Jackson, whose straw-coloured moustache hung down like liana over the mouthpiece of his trombone, always wore a spongeable celluloid collar and no shirt under his suit of green thornproof tweed, with an *I Zingari* tie which he had found in a waste-basket while visiting a friend in the *Pavillon Anglais*.

But, one night as we finished counting the takings, he said abruptly: 'Really, you chaps are a couple of idle scabs, layin' back and drinking yon milk, while I turn meself inside out. Ah'm givin' you a day's notice, as from to-night.'

With rugged Yorkshire business sense, he felt that he was now well enough known not to need an interpreter, and even if he lost a bit on the collection because of the speed through the door of some patrons, it still came cheaper than supporting us. With starvation staring us in the face again, I pleaded with him. He argued back. Finally, I said, 'Look, if we play instruments with you, will you keep us on? The takings would be much bigger.' He stared at me craftily, then said at last, 'Awright, but you'm got to be playing by the end of t'week, or you've 'ad it. An' I want two thirds.'

It so happened that I had some experience with wind instruments. As a Sergeant in the Junior Training Corps, I had fallen under the spell of a verdigrised euphonium which I found in a dark recess of the school armoury. After a lavage with a stirrup pump, it made low, tragic music, as if it had been lonely a long time. But I was just making some progress when one morning Swinhoe Phelan stepped on it under my desk, and gnarled the valve assembly so extensively that the airway was obliterated. Sadly, I put it back in the armoury with a buff form 125c attached which read: 'Euphonia, 1, unrepairable – intussusception at level of sphincter of Oddi.'

Then, under the influence of an ethereal poetess, who held concerts in a lock-up council garage, I had learned to do a vibrato on the recorder. But Tiberio decided that the voice of the latter would be too pitiful alongside the blare of a rug-cutting trombone.

So we hunted about in the antique shops of the Rue Bonaparte, but no bandsmen seemed to have sold their livelihoods that week, and the only offer that we got was the papier mâché horn of an Edwardian phonograph. Finally, just when we were despairing, I found a handsome clarinet going very cheaply in the pawnshop next to the horse butchers in the Rue des Saints-Pères.

Tiberio and I took it back to the *Ecole Agronomique*, and polished up the fingering system with wire wool. Then, fitting a reed, I settled down to master the scales. The things seemed to need industrial amounts of air in order to produce the most elegiac lowing sounds. I could manage an octave in both directions, then had to lie down on the bathroom floor to pant, the purplish mist of anoxia before my eyes.

We had just discovered a blown gasket at the level of the first joint, when there came a knock at the door. It was one of the skull-faced, histrionic Frenchmen from down the corridor. Face drawn with anguish and hand clapped to his prematurely lined forehead, he exclaimed, *'Dieu, que le son du cor est triste au fond des waters'* – a plaintive quotation, I think, from the *Chanson de Roland*.

We had no more complaints that day, but the following one the concierge bustled up and said nastily that if he heard any more of that confounded instrument he would put the lavatory in service again. This was unthinkable. We tried practising in the Jardin du Luxembourg, but the first arpeggio always brought up a horde of children full of the terrifying precocious sagacity of French ten-year-olds.

So we had to rumble out to Versailles in Tiberio's acutely rusty old Renault, ringing a handbell at the intersections as an anti-collision measure. Once there, I aimed the muzzle of the clarinet into a thorn thicket, with Sid Greenbaum's tutor propped up in a scrub oak. Tiberio puffed away into his ceramic ocarina, that could be overblown into a supersonic range that sent nosy dogs yelping away with ear-pain.

In five days, we had a closely woven version of 'Gloomy Sunday' ready, and the 'Peanut Vendor' was coming along well. By the end of the week, as we set out with Jackson for the boîte, I said shyly to him, lapsing easily into musicianly jargon, 'We're digging it with you to-nite.' We were too excited to be downcast when he just replied, 'Two thirds for me then, just you mind.'

We went to a little club which you entered through a sort of coal-hole in the pavement. The proprietor, a big black man from the Cameroons, smilingly introduced us as a threesome. I caught Jackson's eye, untangled my fingers, called, 'A-one, A-two, A-three,' and plunged headlong into 'Gloomy Sunday'. The notes squawked out shrilly in the smoky air. Tiberio was cooing manfully, but Jackson had lowered his trombone and was glaring at me. Showing the whites of my eyes, ears empurpling with the effort, I struggled on. Then Jackson interrupted loudly: "'Ere, what key're you in?' I have certain complete intellectual blind spots; they include algebra – it is manifest insanity to talk of A_2-B_2 having factors; the offside rule in Rugby; the Latin subjunctive; and tonic sol-fa. I relaxed my iron embouchure.

'Key?' I asked helplessly.

'You're in A, that's what,' snarled Jackson, 'Yon thunder-stick's in A, shouldn't wonder. You'll 'ave to transpose.'

'I can't,' I said, shutting my eyes and feeling sick.

'Well then, go away and do bird imitations. You're not playin' wi' me.'

Like dogs, the audience scented fear and incompetence. They began to shout '*Au poteau, la clarinette*,' and '*Qu'est-ce qu'on attend*?' Jackson raised the yawning nozzle of his trombone and blasted off a fortissimo derision as, unemployed and on the verge of tears, Tiberio and I ran for the door.

22

Few remember it now, but the streets of Paris in those days were made infernal by the sound of car horns. You were not thought to be driving properly if you did not give a blast at every intersection, whenever overtaking even a handcart, at every pedestrian and person standing suggestively in a doorway, and at dogs, even when they were determinedly walking in the opposite direction, or having vigorous relations with others.

It was only a few years later that an amazingly determined *Préfet* of the City forbad all this honking, and the cacophony was stilled. For years after, many French drivers did not know what to do with their horn hand, genetically conditioned to constant pushing of the button, and they drove through the streets clapping their palms against the outside of their car door, or even ringing muffin bells and firing alarm pistols.

This inability to give warning of their approach made for great nervousness in the driver population, and I remember for a year or two, *Le Figaro* would be full of accounts of men who had climbed out and fought with their starting-handles after collisions at intersections where both had self-righteously taken a priority.

I found it quite quiet and colourless when I finally went back to Cambridge for the Spring term. Abroad, one always had the feeling that dreadful behaviour would pass unremarked because it would not be understood in a different language. Perhaps the only thing that half-compared with the hilarity of the French student was the behaviour of the son of a Judge in my college who normally took after-dinner coffee with my group of twelve or so. He would encourage us to set fire to his escaping borborygmy with a lighter as it emerged from his trousers. One could quite imagine why the methane flames of Will 'o the Wisps inspired such terror in medieval England.

There had been one acute and chronic problem while in

Paris. Girl friends. Perhaps the fact that so many Parisian girls had recently had their heads shaved during the Occupation for cohorting with German soldiers had inspired a degree of xenophobia and convinced them that the home product was best. Anyway, I had had one or two advances rejected, and felt that fairly drastic action was necessary. In our Cité student circles, there was only one much-coveted girl for every four goatish males, so that it was clearly a waste of time to troll there.

Once, while in the RAF, a fellow airman called Sweeney had shown me his infallible technique for picking up young ladies in strange towns. You just circulated round the streets until you found some young female window dressers at work.

Then, catching the eye of a suitably alert one whose hands were free of rings indicating attachments, you made gestures in sign language to convey that you would come back at her knocking off time, and take her out for a drink.

At first I was scornful about the likely success of this practice, but he demonstrated its efficacy to me towards the end of an afternoon in Liverpool, and by barrack curfew time I think that the girl he had fished out of the display in the window would have married him if he had asked her.

So, one day, feeling lonely, I decided to try the Sweeney technique in Montmartre, and, after a wearying walk, saw a long-legged girl at work in the window of a stationers. To my great surprise, she responded to my romantic tic-tac so favourably that she almost ran out on to the pavement to confirm her availability.

For a moment, I thought that I had mistakenly fallen on a professional, but after she joined me later, discovered that she was just a thoroughly friendly girl called Micheline who happened to be on the rebound. Her immediately past boy friend had also been English, and had apparently convinced her of his right to a *Droit de Seigneur* by showing her the ornate buttons of his blazer which said aristocratically: 'HONI SOIT QUI MAL Y PENSE' because that is what the Royal Army Service Corps buttons used to say.

She was an accomplished guide to Paris, and took me down the Catacombes, among all the blotched skulls of early Christians; up the towers of Notre Dame where Quasimodo had swung, sick with love for Esmeralda, on the bell ropes; to the giant Père Lachaise cemetery to admire the tomb of Oscar Wilde, whose loves were better understood by the tolerant French than the Victorian aristocracy; and into the leguminous scents of the early morning Halles vegetable market.

Back at Cambridge, I was aware that the chatty Micheline, and my interminable conversations with other trogs, had transformed my French, and I resolved to repeat the process in Germany. The opportunity came in the summer of 1949, when I arranged to go to Strasbourg University for one of the foreign students' summer courses.

I had always been fascinated by this Alsatian city since reading Goethe's *Dichtung und Wahrheit* at school. He was at the university there too, and with typical Goethean rigorousness cured himself of a fear of heights by spending several hours 147 metres up the cathedral tower; freed himself of a fear of loud bangs by standing with his back to the curfew drum every night on the city walls waiting for the first crashing drumstick impact; and of a nervousness of churchyards after dark by camping out night after night in the big one on the edge of the town.

Our course was a Babel of nationalities; Spaniards, Italians, Americans on veteran grants, Frenchmen studying German, a Brazilian, and several fellow Englishmen. Some wonderful old academics addressed us. One lecturer, with a beard practically down to his waist, quoted medieval bards to us with tears misting his eyes.

A handsome young American by the name of James Lufkin sat in front of me, listening attentively. I discovered later that he had been a Major in the US Air Force, and a fighter pilot. Forty years later, we are still friends, and I am godfather to his son, also called David.

After a month, the time came for me to check out of the Foyer de l'Etudiant Gallia, and start off my trip across Germany. I was a little nervous, because I had planned to hitchhike all the way across the war-shattered country and on to Vienna through the forbidden Russian zone. Travelling by this primitive means, one is very dependent on the goodwill of the populace.

There were a number of crossing points into Germany for

low-grade civilian traffic, and I hitchhiked north–east up Alsace in order to cross on a British one at Lauterbourg. My first French lift was on the back of a Rene Gillot police motor cycle, ridden with verve by a large motard. At 90 miles an hour on this vehicle with no rear springing, I discovered what a liability it was to have a 60-pound bag on my back.

It was not of the sophisticated metal framed sort that nowadays has become feared in most countries on earth as a symbol of unwholesome backpacking, drug-taking itinerants. The exterior was a long, narrow canvas container, originally designed during the war to house collapsible assault boats. I had brought far too much stuff with me, too, as was my wont. I realized that my shoulders would never be the same again if I accepted too many lifts on motor cycles.

I actually crossed the German frontier on the back of a tractor hauling wood in the local forest. There were British guards at the barrier, and they failed to notice my Gibraltar-issued passport. If they had done so, I would have had to retreat to an embassy somewhere to get a visa.

That day, I got as far as the Rhine, still largely bridgeless, and with the tangled and rusty wreckage of war along the banks. I began to think about where to sleep in this mosquito-ridden area. I had already had the experience of walking confidently up to a small pond to have a wash, when I realized that the water was heaving with swimming adders.

Eventually, exhausted, I settled down in a small clump of pine trees with enough undergrowth to hide me from view. In those days, there were tramps everywhere. They referred to themselves as ODZ, short for *Opfer der Zeit*, meaning 'victim of the times'. Some of them could be quite ugly customers, I knew, so I was concerned not to be too vulnerable while sleeping.

Not by any means for the last time, I passed a notice with a Death's Head on it as I clambered into the thicket. It read starkly: DANGER – UNEXPLODED MINES.

Once in my sleeping bag – a roughly sewn child's blanket inside a mercifully waterproof American Army sleeping bag – I was plagued by whining mosquitoes. They were so bloodthirsty that, if my elbow tensed the poplin of the outside sleeping bag,

169

they would immediately stick their proboscises through the material and start sucking. I spent a miserable night, and awoke stiff, bitten and exhausted. If this is what this adventure is going to be like, I thought, I might as well go home now.

But soon my spirits revived as I was driven by the owner of a small wood company in his Mercedes through the outskirts of Karlsruhe, still largely laid waste by our devoted bombing. My first call was to get some German ration cards, though I very shortly discovered that Germany was in fact much better provided with food than ourselves, and most groceries and restaurants laughed at attempts to hand over coupons.

I plodded out of Karlsruhe down the feeder road to the Munich Autobahn. My first contacts with the population had shown me, greatly to my surprise, that there was no apparent resentment for the English people who had bombed the hell out of them, then bought the favours of their womenfolk for a cigarette or two. Indeed, they were remarkably friendly. The Mercedes driver who had brought me into the City centre had even pressed twenty marks into my hand when we parted company, with a little speech anticipating the Common Market about how we were all Europeans, and we belonged together in friendship and understanding.

My lifts for the day ended with a kind, moonfaced youth in Pforzheim, who offered me the bare metal carrier on his push bicycle. My total weight including sack was well in excess of 200 pounds, and I was rapidly too much for both his back tyre and his calf muscles. We wheeled his flat-tyred bicycle disconsolately back to his little white-painted house, and he gave me his bed for my second night in Germany, while he slept on the floor.

Finally I got to Munich, where I stayed in a youth hostel just outside. This was a disaster in one respect because my backpack was systematically looted while I was out going round the ruined city, and by nightfall I was even poorer and worse equipped than when I set out.

The hostel was governed by a *Jugendherbergsvater* with a rather hysterical temper. A tall American student came back from the town after lights out, and thought he was climbing in through his own dormitory window. Unfortunately, he climbed by mistake into the room occupied by the *Jugend-herbergsvater*, and fell in through the window on top of him. We all jumped out of our sleeping bags as we were woken by the most unmitigated series of death-throe screams, and the *Vater* had to be dragged off the terrified American before he throttled him.

After a few days in Munich, I made my way slowly on down into the glorious green and pine clad country of Upper Bavaria that I already knew so well in my mind's eye from Hans Carossa. Then, in the aimless way that hitchhikers travel when they feel obliged to take an attractive lift in some other direction than they planned, I found myself in the town of Rosenheim. Asking a middle-aged German whether he could direct me to the youth hostel, he answered to my surprise, 'Why, are you looking for somewhere to stay?' When I said that I was, he invited me most warmly to his big flat on the second floor of a tenement building, where he lived with numerous issue, including a very pretty daughter who was married to a bitter young man who had lost an arm in the Russian snows five years before. I settled happily in, particularly because it began to rain as soon as I moved in, and went on, as it does sometimes in mountain country, for a week.

It appeared that the father had been a *Reichsarbeitfuhrer* in something rather sinister, the Todt Organisation, but had somehow contrived to keep alive the Christian ideals of a sect called the *Kolping Familien*, which was why he had taken me in.

It was rather unfortunate for me that the daughter married to the disabled ex-Panzer took a rather noticeable interest in me, and used to follow me into my attic room, smiling wistfully. After a bit, I realized that she in her turn was being stalked by her one-armed mate, and I used to dodge round my truckle bed to avoid anything compromising taking place.

Then, one night, the ex-Panzer began showing me photographs from his time on the Russian front. They included pictures of alleged Russian partisans, faces swollen and purple in death, strung up on trees and telegraph poles. After he had let them sink in, he said slowly, 'I am really sorry that we were never able to get to England. We could have had some fun there too.' I realized that he was getting very tired of my presence in

171

the somewhat overheated family circle, and particularly of his wife's obvious tendency to rub her thigh against mine at the table. Fortunately, the morning after, the clouds suddenly rolled back for the first time in a week, the sun appeared, and I was able to take a hasty farewell, and head off down to the mountains.

Oddly enough, that was not quite the last time that I saw the girl. Months later, I was hundreds of miles away in Konstanz station, and I suddenly heard a shriek of recognition. It was the wife. She raced down the track, flung her arms round me, and burst into tears. Mercifully, the ex-Panzer did not seem to be in evidence, or I think that he would have put his remaining arm to sturdy use.

One day, not far from the irresistibly quaint little town of Wank, I had a bit of luck. As I stood gesturing and imploring lifts from the side of the road, I saw a black Hillman Minx with an open roof and English plates coming slowly my way. Two blond young men were in it, and they politely stopped for me. Perhaps out of a desire to show off, or more likely from sheer habit, I asked them in German if they were going towards Fussen. The driver looked me up and down quizzingly before replying. When he did so, it was to say, 'Don't be bloody stupid – you're wearing British Army socks. You're as English as we are.'

We rapidly got over this abrasive beginning, and I embarked in the Hillman for the next four days of adventures. The driver was Peter Prior, later to become my brother-in-law. He was nine years older than me, and had fought right through World War Two, including scampering as an Intelligence Corps captain up the invasion beaches being showered with rose petals by a 16-year-old French girl who had fallen instantly in love with her liberating angel.

But the story that impressed me most was how, after the Army had crossed the Rhine, Peter had driven into apparently empty countryside for several miles. Being tired as a result of having had little sleep for weeks, and seeing a comfortable-looking and deserted farmhouse, he had parked his jeep in the yard, gone in, lain down on the settee in the living room, and nodded quickly off.

Some time later, he was woken by the stealthy sound of the cellar door opening. A huge German appeared, carrying a sub-machine gun, and with hand grenades clashing at his belt. Peter continued to feign sleep, while a platoon of heavily armed men poured out behind their leader, and came to stand round the solitary British Captain.

Peter sat slowly up, smiled agreeably at this nonplussed but hostile group, then said in the way that a good officer cares for his men, *'Haben Sie gefrühstückt?'* – 'Have you had your breakfast?' He went on to add off-handedly that the country-side was now wholly occupied by the Allies, and if the men would just like to pile their arms in the corner, he would see that they were transported quickly to a suitable prison camp. To his utter surprise, after a moment's hesitation, they complied. It was only later that he discovered that he was miles behind their front line.

Because he had enough of discomfort in the war, during the four days of our journey together, as dusk fell, Peter would stop at a suitably opulent-looking farmhouse, strike an attitude of manly appeal, and deliver a short, prepared speech in German with a Churchillian accent which began, *'Wir sind drei Englische Studenten. Wir machen eine Ferienreise hier in Deutschland . . .'*, before making an appeal for a plot of land to park his commodious tent, followed preferably by breakfast in the morning. He invariably succeeded.

When we got to Lermoos, under the shadow of Germany's tallest mountain, the Zugspitze, nearly 10,000 feet high, we decided to go to the top of the rope railway. The air seemed thin and chilly, and there were incredible numbers of men in Lederhosen and girls in dirndls circulating on the restricted space of the peak because there was a Trachtenfest, or national costume fête, down in the valley.

All went well until the time came to go down. Then when we got back to the top station, there was an orderly queue of hundreds of Schnapps-stimulated, Loden-clad Germans waiting to go down. Peter asked the stationmaster how long the waiting people would take to be shipped valleywards, and he was told that we would have to wait two hours. He was not having that, because it was already nearly dark, and the three of us were already shivering in our light khaki shorts and thin shirts. Peter struck another attitude; *'Wissen Sie mit wem Sie sprechen?'* he demanded haughtily of the stationmaster. The latter, recently defeated, began to cringe; *'Nein,'* he did not know who he was talking to.

'This,' said Peter, pointing to my shivering and praeter-naturally youthful-looking figure, 'is the son of the General.' As all the Germans knew, General Sir Brian Robertson, later to captain British Rail, and at that time Commander of the British Army of the Rhine, was in the town for the fête. Peter went on to snarl that the General would be very unhappy if he knew that his son was being held a virtual prisoner at the top of a freezing mountain by the people that he had so recently defeated.

With great ceremony, pointed at respectfully by the losers-out in the queue, we were escorted into the next car, and sank out of sight down the cliff, followed by the salutes of the stationmaster.

Finally, we went our separate ways with real regret. They were going back to England, and I now had the problem to crack of getting to Vienna. Austria was even more heavily occupied than Germany, mainly because of the presence of the fearsome Russians, who had fanned out in the smiling mountains and valleys as far across the Steyrmark as Linz. And it was well known in the student world that several unfortunate Americans had been picked up hitchhiking across their zone, and were languishing in prison in Sankt Polten.

Intending to slip into Austria via Bregenz, I went on down to the Bodensee, known to us as Lake Constance. A hospitable family of children took me in. They were occupying the Schloss Meersburg with only nannies and gardeners while the grown-ups were away somewhere. I spent a few days inside the ancient walls, once lived in by either Annette Von Droste-Hülsoff or Lulu von Straus und Torney, I forget which. But both poetesses' names are worth mentioning for the euphony. The way that my childish hosts carried on reminds me now of the precocious, upper-class confidence so well described by Nancy Mitford in *Love in a Cold Climate*.

Finally, I left their sunny paradise, with its boats and lakeside beach huts, and hitch-hiked along the shore road, past

174

the Zeppelin town of Friederichshafen to Lindau. The frontier to Bregenz was guarded by dark-uniformed French soldiers. I approached them with confidence, as a member of a fellow Occupying Power, but, after they had studied my passport, the bureaucracy started. My desire to cross to Vienna was examined from all angles in a cluttered office by a captain, as was my lack of a Control Commission visa. Finally, he said, in the manner of functionaries everywhere: '*Non, non et non, Monsieur. Vous n'avez pas le droit de passer,*' and I plodded back down the road into the last German town.

23

I travelled the usual zigzag hitchhiker's route up from Bregenz to a place called Bad Reichenhall, within striking distance of another stretch of the Austrian frontier by Salzburg. In spite of the somewhat better-fed few days with Peter, I was beginning to lose weight rather fast, existing mainly on a diet of stale rye bread and low-grade cheese, varied occasionally by uncooked oatmeal with sugar mixed in it, and fruit when I could pick it without offending anybody.

Finally one day, miles from anywhere in the mountains somewhere east of Kempten, I felt so weak and ill that I crawled into the hay of a barn in a deserted Alpine meadow and stayed there for nearly two days without seeing a soul. Apart from solitude, hunger and thirst, I had one alarming experience; happening to be looking across the meadow one day, I saw a large grey animal making a beeline for my hideout. I gripped a large wooden hayrake which I had kept handy in case any ODZs tried to share the place with me. When, snarling and growling, it tried to leap and scramble the eight feet up to me, I shunted it vigorously back down again several times.

I could not be sure whether it was one of the wolves that I had often heard about. Certainly it was very large, and its eyes were the icy grey that you never see in domestic dogs. But it may just have been someone's freakish Alsation. Anyway, after that I decided that, wobbly-kneed or not, I was going back to civilization.

Clambering stiffly down, I began to walk slowly through the forest to a place called Allhausen which figured on the last sign that I had seen. Suddenly, a farmhouse loomed up among the misty trees. I looked longingly towards the comfortable interior I could glimpse through the window. The farmer's wife must have somehow seen me staggering past because she came out in her apron and called to me, '*Heh, junger Mann,*' then asked if I was all right. I told her that I was far from home, had not eaten for days, and had a wolf after me. With amazing kindness, she ushered me straight into her kitchen and cooked me three fried eggs, liberally spattered with caraway seeds in the curious local culinary tradition. They tasted like ambrosia.

As usual in that peculiar way of life, a day or two later I arrived at the youth hostel near the Königsee, and everything was completely different. I was surrounded night and day by laughing, talking, drinking, reformed ex-Hitler Youth lads, now all thoroughly companionable students in their twenties. One day, I went up with them to Hitler's Adlers Horst, on the top of a nearby mountain above Berchtesgaden. They pushed their bicycles up the dusty white road to the huge pile of wreckage that the British Lancasters had left after they pulped the once-proud mountain-top hideout. I stood on the precarious pile of concrete and reflected that it was less than five years since Hitler had strutted about there with Eva Braun, gazing out over the amazing panorama of cliffs, gorges and lakes.

The Lancs had bombed the road as well, so that, when we started back down with me clinging to the hard carrier of an ex-Wehrmacht bicycle, I had a very uncomfortable ride. There was only a back pedal brake, rapidly becoming red hot, which prevented us from plunging into the abyss on the steep curves. My driver had been in the Panzers at the end of the war, and he set his robust steed at one hastily repaired crater after another, with the dash that he had clearly learned in Normandy.

Finally, he overdid it, and we leapt in the air, landing mercifully back on the tyres. But, because I had soared higher than the rest of the ensemble, we came down with my right foot jammed in the spokes. The machine halted abruptly, and I was lucky not to lose my toes in the mêlée, only a lot of epidermis.

Before I left Bad Reichenhall, I also limped up to a local peak called the Watzmann. The only footgear that I had was some ancient sandals, the hole in one sole being blocked by a cardboard cigarette packet. This drew a stern rebuke from a German Alpinist, who thought it frivolous to circulate on cliffs in something so wretched. As I had waited for him and his wife to scramble down a long chimney above where I stood, followed by another couple, I noted to my surprise that most of the ladies did not seem to be wearing knickers underneath their dirndls. When the German started on my sandals, I reminded myself of the feeble 'knock knock' joke about a certain Nicholas, which ends with the punchline 'Knickerless girls should not climb trees.' I began to splutter with giggles, which convinced him that I was utterly lacking in mountain etiquette. It took an effort of will to start the difficult ascent myself, and stop waiting for more of this mobile peepshow.

Now I was in the American zone, and I hoped that I might be able to benefit from a more relaxed standard of bureaucracy. I moved up to the border on one of the main roads to Salzburg. Noticing that there was a large Yankee camp on the German side, and that streams of officers' wives seemed to be driving in their large cars over the border to shop in the major Austrian town three miles away, I stood craftily gesturing for a lift outside their guardroom.

Soon a kindly mother of two stopped and picked me up, and we covered the few hundred yard to the barrier. Gum-chewing American MPs peered perfunctorily into the big Chevvy at the four of us. I smiled toothily back, as I imagined a rather over-age American child might. Then we were waved on, and I was through.

I stayed in Salzburg long enough to take in a performance of *Jedermann* (Everyman) in the cobbled square in front of the Cathedral, and one of the Fischer-Dieskaus in Antigone rumbling away in front of the cliff at the Felsenreitschule. Then I set off for Linz.

My plan was to move on into the Russian zone by the simple expedient of getting a lift on the back of a lorry, and hiding in its load until it had passed the two controls – one American and one Russian – on the bridge that spanned the Danube. Then, when the lift stopped in Russian-held territory, I would simply carry on in the direction of Vienna, keeping a wary eye out for Red Army patrols. I think that I was rather influenced by all the wartime literature that I had read about escaped prisoners of war.

About two miles short of the bridge, I stopped a lorry that seemed perfect for the job. It had a huge load of cucumbers, and the driver appeared quite unconcerned that I wanted to venture into the Russian zone. I climbed on board, and burrowed into the spiky vegetables so that I could not be seen from the ground.

I felt the vehicle stop while the driver had his papers checked by the usual showily-dressed American MPs, then we ground over the bridge. I could not know it, but relations were bad between the posts at either end apparently because earlier that month the Americans had discovered one day that it was the young Russian guard commander's birthday, and had presented him with a bottle of bourbon whisky as a well-meant present. He was a simple lad from a country village, had never seen whisky before, so gulped the whole bottle in gratitude. Shortly afterwards, he fell into the river and was lost. The Russians had concluded that this was a vile anti-proletariat plot, and had broken off speaking terms.

Now I felt the lorry stop again on the north bank. Voices were raised, which slowly got louder. Eventually, I felt someone rootling about in the cucumbers above my head, and, realizing that the game was up, sat upright. The spectacle that met me was not encouraging. A machine gun was being pointed at my head at short range, wielded by a shrieking Russian soldier who had a complete set of badly fitting stainless steel Red Army teeth, like those popularized subsequently by James Bond's Jaws. The only Russian phrase that I could remember at that moment was '*Zhisn nye shootka*', meaning 'Life is no joke'. This caused a further explosion of rage, from which I inferred that the little man had no sense of the ridiculous. I was dragged down and put under arrest.

Seeing the commotion, one of the American MPs very bravely crossed the bridge. While my Russian captor bared his metal fangs proudly at all and sundry, I explained to the kindly Yank that I was an Ally, and was attempting a harmless journey to Vienna to see some friends. With considerable difficulty, he plucked me from my captors, assured them that I would be punished, and marched me back over the long bridge crossing the swirling dark water.

Once back in his own guardroom, he told me sternly that I had just risked my freedom, and if I tried anything like that again, I would be sent back in a bag to London. Then he clapped his thigh, roared with laughter at the thought of the cucumbers, and broke open a Coke for me. As I left, he said that my best hope was to get a lift over the Semmering Pass by night, as that was the only official crossing point for Vienna, and, if I had the luck to get a lorry that stopped only for the guarded crossing in and out, I might just get through without being arrested.

I decided to try it after consulting my map, and retired back into the town of Linz to begin the journey to the east. The route led along the steep-sided valley of the River Enns, and the rains that had driven me into shelter in Rosenheim had obviously caused the most catastrophic flooding along the banks. This had long subsided, but there were fallen trees and damage everywhere, and vehicles seemed to be avoiding the area. So I had a long walk. Eventually, I fell into step with a fat little bearded man who said his name was Zuschrott, and who proved to be a professor of some obscure linguistic subject. It began to grow dark, and he suggested that I might brighten the life of his sister-in-law, who lived nearby, and who had been lonely ever since her Oberst husband had been shot by the Americans.

I followed him to the lady's dark, gloomy house, which lay up the side of the valley. She seemed grateful for the sound of human voices, and gladly took me in, giving me her husband's study to sleep in for the night. Later, looking idly through his library, which lined one wall, I pulled out a copy of *Mein Kampf*, which was signed with affectionate regards to her husband from Adolf. I began to understand why he had met such a summary fate.

In the morning, after a touching farewell from the sad middle-aged lady, who asked me to stay a bit longer, I plodded on towards Leoben and Eisenerz. The lifts were very thin, but I finally got a short one into Eisenerz with a tall, blond young man who invited me to stay for the night with his equally handsome family called Helfenburger.

His striking-looking sister had a fiancé in tow, who left the house well before bedtime in an affecting show of propriety. I was settled down on the floor of the sitting room, and was just drifting off, thinking of my dash for Vienna on the morrow, when the door quietly opened. I made no move, but quite soon could feel the warmth of another human presence very close to me. It was the sister. 'I just came to see if you were lonely,' she murmured softly. 'You can't imagine how lonely,' I said, really meaning it. 'So am I,' she whispered. I felt her hands, stroking my face in the darkness, and was just about to rear out of my sleeping bag and take the situation firmly in both hands when the door suddenly opened, the light came on, and the brother stood there. There was a moment of French farce, because I could now see that the girl was wearing almost nothing.

'Yes, I thought I would find you here,' said the brother sternly, 'now go to your room, and don't you dare leave it until morning.'

She left hurriedly, a succulent female package viewed from behind. 'I'm so sorry,' said the brother, 'she gets carried away.'

'I'm sorry too,' I said, with fervour. I had a bit more difficulty in getting to sleep after that.

The following day, the Helfenburger family said nothing about the night's events to me, although I seemed to detect a certain stiffness in their attitude, as if I now possessed some unwelcome information about them all. I was glad to get back on the road towards the pass.

Lifts were slow in coming, and I was obliged to walk miles. Finally, I found another hitchhiker, a pretty girl a few years older than myself who had served in the Luftwaffe, and who was also trying to cross the Russian zone to get to Vienna. Hiding behind her, both of us rapidly got a lift on a Hungarian lorry loaded with newsprint that was grinding up the incline towards the pass. Predictably, the driver took the girl in the warm cab with him, leaving me to fend for myself, clinging to the old tarpaulin that covered the rolls of paper.

It was getting quite late, and, as we got slowly higher, having left the British and Russian frontier posts behind, a light rain began to fall. I cowered down into the deepest hollow I could find, freezing cold and very uncomfortable. Suddenly, there was a ripping sound, and a seam collapsed, letting me sink down into the relative protection of a layer of the thick fabric. The lorry roared on and on. Finally, we reached the top of the pass, at something over 4000 feet. Suddenly we stopped, and the driver's door banged as he got out. I was a bit afraid that he might think that I had deliberately ripped the fabric in order to carve out a shelter, so I tried to struggle out before he could see me inside it. But he had obviously suspected something because he was up on his tailboard in a flash, roaring accusations in strongly accented German at me that I was a hooligan, and now I could get off, right there in the Russian zone, and jolly well walk.

There did not seem to be a house for miles, and I was very alarmed at the prospect. Then, to my great relief, there was another intervention. The ex-Luftwaffe girl jumped down from the other side of the cab, and shouted, 'Please don't throw him off. If you'll let him stay up there, I'll be nice to you when you get back into the cab.'

With equal suddenness, he calmed down, they both got in without another word, and I cowered back into my inadequate shelter. Presently, the lorry rumbled on, reaching the suburbs of Vienna at about 2 o'clock in the morning. The driver stopped, shouted that I must now get down, and the girl climbed off as well. It was then that I got my next surprise. She put her arm through mine, and said, 'Now you can show me your gratitude by buying us a room at the Südbahnhof Hotel.' I did as she asked, although buying the setting for the remarkable experience that I had next took every cent that I still had on me for the rest of my journey. And I realised for the first time, as the Duke of Edinburgh was to say later in *Encounter*, that a pretty girl is sitting on a gold mine.

In the morning, I staggered out past the head-wagging porter, and caught a tram to the diplomatic quarter with my last few groschen. It was a strange change of pace – to be graciously received by the Commercial Counsellor of the British Embassy and his charming and elegant family. I had known his son Peter both at school, and also up at Cambridge. University gossip had it that Peter, all six foot four of him, spent his vacations in Vienna, tracking Werewolves, as Nazi survivors were called. His favourite method of observing them was said to be watching their movements from telephone boxes through slits in that day's copy of *The Times*. During my stay, I did not find any evidence of this, although he undoubtedly had some covert role there.

Shortly before, he had married a strongly built Russian ballet dancer. It took me a few days to realize that she still longed for Mother Russia, and meanwhile I unwittingly caused great offence by excitedly telling the stories that Austrians had told me about their Soviet masters. How they would go to the doors of houses demanding porcelain chamber pots to send home to their families for cooking vegetables, how they would requisition bicycles from passing cyclists, then proceed to fall off them, first on one side, then on the other, until they were out of sight. And how they would cheerfully drink petrol and antifreeze on party nights when the vodka ran out.

Peter's wife thought that I was being grossly unfair, making fun of simple country boys who had nothing at home, and whom the war had forced to leave their villages for the first time in their lives and she suddenly burst out at lunch to say so. After that I avoided all reference to the occupying forces, because I had been told that, once at breakfast with her husband, he had offended her; whereupon she had picked up everything that was on the table – coffee pot, marmalade, eggs and bacon, butter and so on – in the folded cloth, and dumped the whole issue on his head.

Happily eating Sacher cakes with the hospitable family, and dining on the heights of the Danube with a fabulous view of the city, I rapidly regained half a stone, and, after a week, I felt quite different when I came to stand at the side of the road out of Vienna, to hitchhike back through the Russian Zone.

24

Even after months of wandering and living on my wits, the Moreau family gene that carries the desire to travel continuously had still not had quite enough. I could have gone straight back to the Channel Ports, after an honourable eight weeks of my vacation spent on the road, often in conditions of real hardship. But I was learning so much German, meeting so many people, and having so many adventures that I decided to go back in a huge loop that would take in both Switzerland and Italy.

I had never been to Switzerland before, and crossed the frontier at Schaffhausen. It had not really occurred to me how used I had become to seeing battlefield cripples and war-shattered villages – some of the latter still with their main water supply provided by a few standpipes among the shells of houses – until I met the geranium-covered neatness and tranquillity of the Swiss towns and hamlets. Ancient, ginger wooden houses, with well-nourished, apple-cheeked occupants, and never a bullet hole or an artificial limb in sight.

They were conscious, too, when I talked to them, that they had done their level best to help in the conflict via the Red Cross, food parcels, taking in starving children and escaped Allied prisoners, without getting involved in the actual fighting. In many ways, their contribution had been much greater than if their tiny population had thrown its slender weight in on our side. Later, I was to go to Sweden, where it seemed to me that the guilt left over from helping and encouraging German barbarism for the first two years of the war could remain for generations.

A family called Toggenburg gave me a lift out of Schaff-hausen towards their native town of Winterthur. For accommodating strange young hitchhikers, they had the ideal profession – they manufactured horsehair mattresses. I decided that it was not for nothing that the Swiss were the world's best hoteliers, particularly when Mr Toggenburg gave me a pair of solid leather sandals which were to last me summer and winter for the remainder of my time in Cambridge.

I moved on across the country. Deciding to go to Italy over the Gotthard, I plodded up the foothills. In those days, the sophisticated tunnel that cuts out the need to go up to over 7000 feet through the village of Andermatt had not even been thought of. Finally, I got a lift in a gleaming three-and-a-half litre SS Jaguar, that had spent its whole war on blocks in a garage, to emerge resplendently gleaming afterwards and bear its ex-Colonel owner on the sort of grand touring that he had dreamed of during a hard war in a county regiment.

As we climbed higher, it began to grow dark. And because there was already an autumnal dampness in the air, a heavy mist reflected back our huge headlights. Soon it became a fog, and my gallant driver could see almost nothing as we came in to the unending serpentine bends. We feared that we might go over the edge, for Armgard had not been invented, and the best protection available to stop you tumbling down the precipices was the line of grey granite blocks that stood at ten yard intervals like milestones along the edge of the abyss.

So I volunteered to get out and run in front of the car in the freezing darkness, making hand signals as I dimly saw which way the next bend went. I must have covered several miles like this, before the gradient slackened, the fog lifted, and I could see the lights of Airolo in the valley below.

We parted in Bellinzona. I asked a passer-by if there was a youth hostel, and he shook his head, then suggested that the monastery, dimly visible up the side of the valley, would take me in. Beginning to tire, I struggled up there. When I swung on the bell, like the sort of thing film-makers put outside Dracula's castle, and with a similar clangour inside, an old monk shuffled to the door. He spoke only an Italian dialect, so, for the first time since I left prep school, I was grateful for the drilling in Latin by Cassivelaunus Wilhelm Musgrave Burtley which enabled me to ask politely for a bed.

I was shown to a whitewashed cell, which, rather to my surprise, had quite a comfortable bed under a giant bronze crucifix. Kindly monks dropped by from their cells to make sure that I was comfortable and had everything that I needed. They had the engaging childishness and tendency to giggle of grown-up children. I became slightly nervous when they showed no sign of going when I said I was going to bed, so, with memories of the School Chaplain, and of a Seaman's Hostel where I had once unwisely spent the night while in the RAF, I went ostentatiously to bed fully clad.

In the morning, I was shown the wine-making and cheese-making department, and the remainder of the offices where they lived in a style which had scarcely altered since the Middle Ages. Then I set out for Locarno. I realized that I was beginning to feel a bit lack-lustre about the struggle that life presented every day, and it might be prudent to cut out most of the proposed trip to Italy because I knew from others that the war had left behind a tradition of minor crime which would mean that sleeping rough and travelling at a subsistence level would probably be even more dangerous than elsewhere.

Domodossola had a legendary status in the family, because it was there that my parents had spent happy hours on their honeymoon watching Buzzards, Spotted Eagles and other raptors through their binoculars.

As I stood gazing about me just outside the town, wondering whether to make a dash for the Simplon Pass in the evening, an odd, swarthy-faced character rode up on a woman's bicycle, addressing me in fractured English. He told me that his name was Obergottesberger, and that he was a cousin of the British Royal Family.

Rather unwisely, I agreed that I needed shelter for the night, and followed him up the winding track to his house, which had a marvellous view in both directions over the valley and the Lepontine Alps.

Soon, an Italian youth appeared from nowhere, thundering up to the long, low house on an ancient Norton motor cycle. The two of them settled down to the haphazard cooking of a series of Italian dishes based on pasta, and the consumption of formidable amounts of red wine. I think that they had in mind getting me plastered, and not for the first time I was grateful for the military efficiency of my liver, whose enzymes attacked and cracked up the alcohol molecules almost as they arrived. Thus, in spite of frenzied refilling of my glass as soon as I sipped out of it, I was able to watch in relative sobriety as they sank slowly under the table.

A turbulent night followed. Obergottesberger kept appearing in my room, egged on by Mario, the Italian, usually behind him on his hands and knees. The Royal cousin would be shouting incoherently, like a Latin Lady Macbeth. Then, at his last appearance at about 5.30 a.m., like many drunks, he had turned nasty as the sobering up process began and his blood sugar plummeted. He announced that I must go immediately, as I was not a sport like the young Frenchmen, Dutchmen, and Germans that usually drank with them and passed out, or perhaps became more co-operative.

The previous night, before it got dark, I had noticed a rough track which led away along the top of the ridge in the direction of the Simplon Pass. I decided to follow it, cutting off a corner on the long ascent to 7000 feet.

I had been going for about an hour, watching the sun coming up slowly and magnificently, when I felt a call of nature. It seemed natural in that wilderness to lower my tattered shorts, sit on the tumbledown wall at the side of the track, and suspend my backside over a drop of 1500 feet to the boulder-strewn valley below.

I was ruminating in this posture, when I heard the crunch of a soft footfall on the gravel just round the bend in the track 25 yards away. Unable to move, I saw at least thirty teenage girls in the care of several grim-faced nuns walking briskly towards me. They passed close enough to me for their black habits to brush my knees, while I smiled sicklily at them all, and croaked responses to their cheeky, knowing cries of *'Buon giorno, Signor.'* I never discovered where they were bound, nor where they had come from.

I got back to Cambridge just in time for the restarting of the Michaelmas term, and badly in need of a rest. But I had achieved my object: both the French and the German examiners gave me Distinctions in the oral exams that came right at the beginning of the term. Captain Austin, the ex-marine senior porter at my college, was so moved at the glory that this reflected on the College that he forgave me his annoyance at a previous roof-climbing incident, during which Armstrong-Jones and I had left an array of white pots twinkling in the early morning sun on the College Chapel roof, and he spent what seemed like minutes pumping my hand.

Trevor Jones, who was one of the examiners, said afterwards that, if he had not been so dazzled by my wholesale grasp of blasphemous and semi-lavatorial modern German slang, he would have noticed that my grammar still had a proletarian inexactitude. I explained that this was not surprising because the only upper class lift that I had had was with Baron Von Flotow and his family, and otherwise I had related only with lorry drivers and peasant farmers.

After the three absorbing months of a day and night panorama, during which I often felt that I was on a stage as I learnt how to make progressively more complex jokes in a variety of languages, Cambridge seemed more pedestrian than ever.

My County Major scholarship from Wiltshire totalled £168 per year, and my father had no spare cash to make any contribution. The only extra money was my pathetic earnings as a harvester, blackberry picker and amateur postman. So that I had no cash for anything extra. I knew that membership of the Cambridge Union was essential to guarantee a golden future, but the £7 entrance fee was beyond me. Norman St John Stevas was President at the time that some charitable member took me in to watch a debate, and I saw this dark-haired, evening-suited figure urbanely dominating the discussion and firing off witticisms just as I was sure, in a couple of decades, he would be doing in the Mother of Parliaments.

I think that my real poverty must have kept me from one or two other activities that I would have dearly loved. For example, I still wanted to learn to fly, and I could probably have done so for nothing in the University Air Squadron. But, because an existing member told me that there were a number of expenses involved, I shied away from the idea, and learned to fly at my own expense years later. In fact, I think that he was not correct.

But one of my other obsessions, acting, was definitely

affordable because it cost nothing. My ability to reproduce the sounds of my Wiltshire friends of yesteryear got me parts as shepherds, messengers and lumpkins in various University and College performances of Coventry Mystery Plays and bucolic comedies. I also rejoiced in playing doddering old men with loose false teeth, and Italians whose voice boxes had been scoured by grappa and hand-rolled cigarettes.

I had heard – probably also wrongly – that the Footlights Club was riddled with poofters, so that non-brethren had to keep their backs to the wall when performing there. As I had suffered enough in this respect, I refused an invitation to join and try out my modest talents there.

Then I had an audition at the ADC, Cambridge's premier amateur theatre. Like many small-time character actors, I had always nourished a desire to play Laurence Olivier-type romantic leads. I had chosen a speech of this sort from some long-forgotten play, and thundered it out with a wealth of extravagant gestures to the unimpressed audience of the committee, whose unanimous opinion at the end was that I should stick to old men and ethnic yokels.

One of the plays that I enjoyed most in these low-profile roles was the First Gravedigger in a certain Geoff Darby's perform-ance of Hamlet. I could see the spectacles of the *Sunday Times* critic Harold Hobson shining in the front row. Mark Boxer, as nervous as a kitten, played Polonius with his voice shaking for real. Sir Peter Hall had the role as the Player King, fore-shadowing perhaps the half lifetime that he has spent ordering his troupes about. The gloomy priest, hooded and unrecogniz-able, was acted on successive nights by different luminaries, including John Barton, who for years since has captained the Shakespeare Theatre at Stratford-on-Avon; Julian Slade, later to write *Salad Days*; and Peter Wood, whose name I have often seen since in West End programmes.

The ADC showed me in perfect miniature how the star system worked, and its effect on human personalities. If, for example, while applying your Leichner in the dressing room, you told what you knew to be a screamingly funny story, you were liable to provoke a silence during which pins could be heard dropping to the stained boards from every make-up table. If one of the local stars made a comic remark, sycophantic hysteria would envelope the place.

Rowing was a much more straightforward activity. Because Jesus College had such a reputation in those days, consequent on the activities of their famous Australian coach Steve Fairbairn – it provided most, if not all, of the Olympic boat of 1948, I believe – I had felt obliged to join the Boat Club. It seemed likely that the choking exhaustion at the end of a long race on the Cam would mark our physiques for life, but I nevertheless had one most exhilarating experience. Ours was the Third Jesus Boat, but in the Lenten Races one year, it became the only such lowly craft in history to bump the back ends of four First Boats from other colleges, and thus end up in the First Division. After that, I retired, and took up tennis.

The Final Exams in Modern Languages came and went, leaving me with a BA degree. This involved me in wearing a much longer gown. By now, I was on to motor cycles of my own, and, after an impotent little 150 c.c. BSA, I bought a fearsome 350 racing bicycle with a high compression JAP engine. The Proctors had given me permission to bring this red monster up to Cambridge, and I used to ride it between lectures. One morning, I was thundering my way beyond Parker's Piece to a lesson. Somewhere opposite Christ's College, as I was accelerating hard, the gown caught in the chain and back wheel. It curled up instantly, like a roller blind, dragging me off backwards. I can remember the terrible feeling as my left hand came off the clutch lever, and I had no further control as my hand had already been wrenched off the throttle on the other side of the handlebars.

I was not, of course, wearing a helmet, because only Army dispatch riders wore them then. With a sickening thud, reported to me with a relish by a bystander afterwards, the top of my head hit the road backwards.

I woke up on the operating table at Addenbrookes Hospital five hours later. A young doctor, seeing me stirring, asked repeatedly whether I could remember what had happened, and there was general relief when I told him. I had half-bitten my tongue off, there were a number of scrapes on me, and I had a click in my jaw which is with me still forty years later. But, apart from a tendency for the room to spin round when I lay down at night, there were no permanent ill-effects. The Proctors sent me a message chiding me for taking the gown-wearing instructions so literally. After twenty-four hours in the hospital, I got tired of all the prostatic old men round me, and resolutely dressed and discharged myself.

As I walked slowly and carefully across Market Hill, I saw my Tutor, the distinguished lawyer R. Y. Jennings, now Sir Robert, coming in the opposite direction. He blenched visibly at the sight of me, then said that he had understood that I was seriously injured, and had just sent for my parents to come and sit at my bedside.

Other fears now loomed. What was I going to do with the rest of my life? My father, with his respect for public service, had long thought that I ought to go into the police or the Diplomatic Service, and I had promised him that I would do the necessary exam for the latter in due course. He had an aversion to company directors, and, indeed, had had one or two experiences with bent ones that made this understandable. So that for a time I thought that, to prevent family discord, it might be unwise to go into commerce.

Soon, the effort of trying to choose a career was too much for me, and, although most of my friends had suddenly gone down and moved into gainful occupations, I decided to stay at Cambridge and take another Tripos, this time in Law. My father thought that I was being a bit frivolous, but finally agreed that it might be useful to have a lawyer of sorts in the family.

25

The ending of my time at Cambridge still had some rare moments. There was a May Ball, and, penniless as I was, I had decided to enjoy it in the same way as previous years – by waiting ticketless in a room in College dressed in someone else's old dinner jacket until things had really got under way, then quietly emerging and mingling. There were always a few chaps who had passed out cold, leaving their carefully groomed girl friends to mill round aimlessly looking for shoulders to cry on.

But this time, a strange thing had happened; the housekeeper at Girton had befriended a German girl, whom she had imported to Cambridge to get her away from her ruined homeland for a stint, and this kind lady made enquiries round the College for a senior student who was a German speaker, and could be relied on not to try to tumble her protegée in the first few minutes of acquaintance.

I was approached, and she pressed two free tickets into my hand. I waited for the girl with some anxiety, but she mercifully proved to be wholesome and generally well put together. We danced rather stiffly for a bit, trying to find subjects in common, then I heard that someone had lost his girl friend to another reveller in the course of the evening, so had decided to become fighting drunk in the beautiful old Ghost Room upstairs in the Cloisters. Unable to resist the spectacle, we went round and stood at the bottom of the stairs, as one irate porter after another came tumbling down the steep staircase, accompanied by thuds and roaring sounds from upstairs. I found it all quite jolly as a cabaret, but for some reason that I could not fathom, it frightened the life out of my German companion, and she burst into tears, remaining weeping for the rest of the evening, despite all efforts to distract her with everything from boyish passion to bottle after bottle of other people's wine.

I am afraid that my free May Balls were not the only debts of honour that I left behind. A good friend of mine called Tony Taylor and I used to go to dances at the Dorothy Hall on most Saturday nights. One of us would pay a ticket and go in legitimately, then unobtrusively open the windows behind the long curtains, so that a stream of dishevelled undergraduates could then climb in, including one or other of us. The curtains would heave silently for a bit, until the lights lowered, and we could escape one by one in waltz time.

Going to the Law School every day, very recently vacated by such people with a future as the young Sir Geoffrey Howe and Judge Oliver Popplewell, I found the subject a storehouse of unpredictable yarns, particularly in Tort.

There was Chaffee, the man who single-handedly provoked the Vexatious Actions Act of 1898 by suing 48 people in two years, including the Archbishop of Canterbury and the Lord Chancellor. And Regina versus Brown, the case in which an East Anglian yokel ended up appealing to the House of Lords to have a conviction for sodomy with chickens set aside because a bird was not an animal, and sodomy was only possible with the Higher Orders, not birds. And the terrible case of a hearse that was hit by a tramcar, which caused ejection of the corpse from its coffin, so that it rolled across the sidewalk and lay with a rictus on its face at the feet of an unfortunate and pregnant Liverpudlian girl, who promptly had a miscarriage, then sued the tramcar company. Very properly, the damage was ruled to be too remote, as the tram driver could not have foreseen the ultimate consequences of his action in wiping the hearse off the road. Or the case of Donoghue and Stevenson, where a distressed drinker found the decaying remains of a snail in the bottom of his stone ginger beer jar. Or Carlile and the Carbolic Smoke Ball Company, where a chap anxious to avoid the flu bought a Smoke Ball, followed the instructions minutely, but nevertheless caught the disease, and just about died from it. Was there a breach of contract there? the Court asked earnestly.

Bursting with all this information and much more, I faced the examiners, and got an upper second in Law to add to the language one.

Somehow, whilst tittering with the rest of my year over the fact that one of our senior Contract Law dons had run away with the wife of the licensee of the Red Cow, I became aware that there were scholarships available to go and study flamenco dancing in Southern Spain. Attempting to delay indefinitely my entry into real life, I applied for one, then told my father what I had done.

He clearly saw his son growing older and more work-shy, and told me so with the forcefulness of one who had been born in the Protestant ethic of the Victorian era. I riposted by pointing out that I had not cost him a penny in the five years since I was eighteen so what difference did it make to him? Nevertheless, I decided not to ruffle the paternal feathers any further, and regretfully declined the sum offered for learning to do a zapateado, and how to hoarsen and coarsen the voice when singing to the specially strident guitar. The immediate problem then became urgent: What to devote my life to for the next sixty years?

I did a small inventory of my abilities; on the negative side, I was neither very handsome nor grotesquely ugly. I was neither tall nor short. I could act a bit, but I was not of star quality. I could write a bit, but I did not come of a writing dynasty, and had been slow to spread into University print, as opposed to the College magazine, which latter I had also illustrated fairly crudely.

With regard to literary dynasties, I one day had a brief exchange with Reresby Sitwell, who was in King's. 'What will you be doing when you go down, Reresby?' I asked rather naively. 'Oh, scribbling, like the rest of us. Y'know, family business, and all that,' he answered with a deprecating wave.

I could play 'Greensleeves' quite well on the clarinet, 'Gloomy Sunday' on the piano, and several Burl Ives hits on the guitar, accompanying them in a tenor voice with an abnormally small range of about five easily-obtained notes.

I knew that I was very quickly bored, and, if something was sufficiently uninteresting, I might go into one of the daydreams that I inherited from my mother, and from which I would have to be roused perhaps hours later. As an inheritance from my father, I could easily go to sleep in lectures or meetings, which really precluded any sort of committees, or even perhaps Parliament itself.

And, finally, I had never been very good at observing the rules about anything, whether in traffic, in human relations, or on games fields.

I had a very loud voice, developed during my days as a sergeant, but, when making public speeches in it, tended to behave like Lord Tweedsmuir's friend in the Union during his major speech there – suddenly yawning because he found himself so boring.

Also, I had developed rather primitive Genghis Khan-type political attitudes, on which it would be hard to base a career in Government. Pat Jenkins, a fellow student in Jesus, and later to become the Patrick Jenkins who, as a Thatcher Minister, humbled Ken Livingstone and the Greater London Council before retiring exhaustedly back into private life, had already begun to disappear on speaking engagements for fellow undergraduates like Pip Jebb who were standing for Parliament. I knew that I would be incapable of feeling strongly enough about the right things to do that.

On the positive side, I could now pass as either a Frenchman or a German. So I thought that I had the stuff of a secret agent in me. We were aware that unmarked individuals were moving smoothly among the undergraduates, stocking up the Intelligence services. An acquaintance of mine in Queens' had recently been taken on, but he would only tell me that someone had struck up a conversation with him at the counter of a pub, and one thing had led to another, and now he had a pensionable job for life. It must be remembered that this was before Burgess, Maclean, Blunt and others had robbed Cambridge of its reputation for heterosexual patriotism, and Donald Bevis was still cheerily appearing in ADC reviews dressed as a schoolgirl. So I paid particular attention to tall dark strangers in pubs, without, however, receiving anything more than some rather peculiar looks.

My other talents were hardly meal tickets either; I was effortless on a brakeless bicycle, weaving at 30 m.p.h. through dense crowds in the Senate House Passage. I could plough a field with five furrows at once, or drive a combine harvester all day. I could probably have swum about halfway across the Channel before sinking. With a revolver, I could break bottles predictably at twenty-five yards. And I could gurn so frightfully that children in pushchairs in department stores would explode into tears at the sight of me behind their mothers' backs.

One day, I happened to be in the Beith Modern Language library, and confided to the librarian, whom I knew well as a motor-cycling oddball, that I was having difficulty in finding a life's work to turn my hand to. To my surprise, he said, 'Well, perhaps this will cheer you up.' From his desk, he pulled out an Ordnance Survey map of the Thames Valley round Henley. It was covered in black dots made with a pen. 'What on earth is the significance of those marks?' I asked.

He looked at me sombrely. 'Guess. It's a practice intelligence test,' he said.

'I can't imagine.' I answered, quite baffled.

'This is a document of the utmost sociological importance,' he said, 'it represents every spot where I have had intercourse with my mistress, who is the wife of another.'

'I don't think that there's a career there,' I said.

Weeks of anxious examination of my navel got me nowhere, so I went along to the Appointments Board to see what they could suggest. Perhaps I looked literary or dissolute, because when I entered the room, Paul Sinker, Head of the Board and a don in my own college, looked up and said, 'Before you ask, Moreau, all the jobs in wine and publishing have already gone. And all the jobs at ICI and Shell have gone to this year's crop of Firsts.'

I said that I had not even considered any of them.

'Well, what sector have you decided to ornament?' he asked.

I thrashed about. 'I shall be taking the Foreign Service exam shortly,' I said, 'if I fail that, I shall need a back-up in, say, motor engineering, the BBC or aircraft.'

It must have been a pretty dreadful job, trying to help men and women who had got as far as I had in life without really experiencing any kind of vocation. He did the best he could for me, sending me down to Dowty, the aircraft hydraulics company, near Tewkesbury, and up to the BBC to be tested for the Monitoring Service at Caversham.

Then I took the Foreign Service exam in a huge hall in Imperial College. It started slowly with general papers and hours of intelligence tests, then built up to a crescendo in a rambling house in Chesham Place. We were shown a series of photographs of scantily-clad boys and girls, and asked which of them we liked best. As a means of detecting those with homosexual tendencies, this was so transparent that I was not surprised that a few years later a large percentage of the service proved to have slipped through into the field despite a left hand thread.

You could tell quite early on who had the urbanity and easy charm to get in. Several of the names of my competing contemporaries turn up in the newspapers regularly, including one of the Bullock dynasty, who came first out of the 1200 of us. I seem to think that I came about 26th, but that was not high enough to qualify.

I remember the subsequent interview with the Civil Service Commissioners for two reasons. Firstly, one of the seven people concentrating on me bowled a low ball by asking me if I had read the obituary of Sir Harold Nicolson in *The Times*. I said that I had, and dilated a bit on his career, only to discover later that he was still vigorously alive. Then I noticed that one of the two ladies kept ducking under the circular table, which was shaped like a giant lavatory seat, with a hole in the middle. Finally, I realized that she was keeping an eye on what I was doing with my feet, hands and legs out of sight of the rest of them.

I was neither disappointed nor elated when I failed to get into the Diplomatic Service. Like the police, it had been my father's idea in the first place, and I had never really seen myself neatly suited and stiff-upper-lipped in foreign parts, achieving a notorious anonymity.

Finally, I went for an interview with a strange company called Meibaum (1948) Ltd in Park Street, Mayfair. They specialized in stiffening collars, cuffs and shirtfronts in a durable way, and derived their not inconsiderable cash flow from selling their process and primitive machines to shirt-makers all over the world, particularly in underdeveloped countries. The size of the down payment was substantial enough to make it fairly irrelevant whether they subsequently paid any more royalties.

George Meibaum, who dominated the whole operation, interviewed me in a glacial way, speaking with a slight German accent. He spoke with real passion of stiffening collars, and I was later to recognize that the first step to making a fortune is undoubtedly to be seized with a deep conviction that your product, even if absurd or trivial, is of overwhelming importance to you and civilization.

To my surprise, towards the end of the interview, he made me an offer of the job of assistant manager with the unimaginable sum of £500 a year as a salary, and I gratefully accepted. That was the start of a strange relationship that lasted a year.

Sometimes when I was dictating, the door of my office would open soundlessly, and the dolicocephalic Meibaum, who always wore soundless crepe-soled shoes, would look lugubriously in. It was on one of these occasions that our previously merely uncomfortable relationship became a feud.

Noticing one day that my hair was beginning to thin in the stress of business, and being under the influence at the time of a girl who believed absolutely in Yoga, I developed my own method of bringing more richly nutritive blood into my scalp. I would kneel on my desk facing the chair, and slowly lower my head on to the deliciously resilient Tan Sad seat. Once there, in the attitude known to surgeons as the lithotomy position, I would do a series of rapid rotatory movements on the corduroy to foster vasodilatation. It was quite similar to the headstanding so recommended by Yehudi Menuhin at the time.

On one occasion, when I was having a particularly prolonged therapeutic session, Meibaum said sadly from just behind me, 'Mr Moreau, I fear that you have taken leave of your senses.' As usual, he spoke as if his whole buccal cavity was made of damp cardboard. I struggled up, accidentally kicking a shower of paper clips at him, red faced and dishevelled. I began to explain, but Meibaum detested excuses, and, gloomily shaking his head, he left me.

I am not quite sure why he thought that this behaviour was so irresponsible. Like many great men, he had his foibles and some of them were not dissimilar. His secretary, Miss Alexander, told me that sometimes, still dictating, he would vanish under his desk. For a while, muffled words continued to emerge, followed by a heavy silence. Then, after a while, he would cross the office floor to his chocolate cupboard, moving easily on his hands and knees. Miss Alexander thought that he did this as an excuse to look up her skirt, but I thought that it was more likely a hypoglycaemic syndrome.

More sinister was his love for searching desks and waste-paper baskets. After a tip-off, I always left my desk at night with the drawers sealed with a tiny sliver of sticky tape. This showed that I was searched at least twice a week. At first, I thought that it was funny to leave notes in the drawers saying such things as: 'MEMO: Warn Mr Meibaum that Lord Attlee told me last night of his plans for nationalizing the commanding heights of Meibaum (1948) Ltd under the next Socialist Government.'

But these little sallies further worsened our relationship, and he took to shaking his head every time that he saw me. The strange thing was that I was succeeding wildly in relieving innocents of large sums of cash, and the post often brought letters from Japanese, Indians, Ghanaians and Fijians saying how wonderfully I had explained how they were to get rich. These came through with Meibaum's initials on them, and no further comment.

But open war was not declared until the Barcelona episode. It so happened that I wanted to motor cycle to Spain for my holiday, and also that, for tax reasons, Meibaum needed to open another branch of the company in Andorra. He happened to be away at one of our counting houses in Liechtenstein when I thundered off, but I did my part in the remote Pyrenean republic, far from our rapacious Inland Revenue, then went on to see a rich new Meibaum customer who lived in a dignified villa on the Costa Brava.

I had taken with me a few prototypes of new Meibaum products, developed by the mad Hungarian scientist that he kept in the basement. One, when put out on the clothes line with the washing, rang a loud bell if it started to rain. It was also perfect for bedwetters. Another was a dramatically effective hair tonic, which had only one side effect; the new growth of hair was snow white.

The Spanish industrialist was delighted to call a press conference to talk about these and his new stiffening agreement with Meibaum, and my picture appeared in the local paper, described as an 'inventor of genius'. I thought that this was a bit exaggerated, but good public relations all the same for both the company and myself. Unfortunately, a copy of the paper preceded me home by about a fortnight, so that Meibaum, who obviously felt threatened by my breezy way of going on, was able to meet me stonily in the hallway on my triumphal return with the single word, 'Exhibitionist', spoken as one might unmouth a piece of gristle.

Because every achievement seemed to make matters worse, I became rather concerned about my future, so I began to look in the Situations Vacant for another job. As usual at the time, most ads seemed to be for versatile doctor–accountant–electronic scientists. Then, a prominent insertion in a box in the columns of the *Economist* caught my eye. It was undoubtedly offering my own job, which was dressed up to sound delectable. It even gave the company's name, which nowadays from the ACAS point of view would be a thumping constructive dismissal, summarily punishable. And when I looked in the *Daily Telegraph* and *The Times*, there it was again.

After a moment's reflection, I drew up a list of all the men and women in London whom I considered to be on my side. Then, I began to telephone them. Almost all of them agreed to make applications for my job, inventing their curriculum vitae, age, parity, marital status and ambitions with great freedom and imagination.

The following day, scrawled letters began to arrive for Meibaum from Austrian counts, Chelsea Pensioners, cooks general, school monitors, even one from the then legendary Messina brothers, superstar brothel-keepers of the time, all offering their services to replace me as export manager.

Meibaum and his lady graphologist – handsomely paid by the hour – sat upstairs, boggling at the bizarre response, and trying to choose a shortlist from a group, nearly none of whom sounded normal. Practically no one turned up, either. When one or two genuine candidates did so, the receptionist quickly rang me, and I ran down to explain in an urgent whisper, interrupted by sobs, that it was my job that was going down the Swannee, and my wife and numerous kids would be going hungry if they persisted with their candidature. To my surprise, casting anxious looks all round them, without exception they left hurriedly.

Looking back, Meibaum did me a favour with his surreal behaviour, because I went swiftly from there into a series of medical companies, to wallow for nearly thirty years in the science that I had been deprived of when Burnwell dragged me round the chemistry lab by the hair. And he taught me a lesson that I have never forgotten, even though I have often paid for ignoring it: modern business is a homicidal affair where it is not only dangerous to fail. It may be even more job-threatening to succeed. Hence the suspended animation below the parapet in which millions of Organization Men feel obliged to pass their blameless lives.